JOBS FOR ALL

A Plan for the Revitalization of America

by
Sheila D. Collins
Helen Lachs Ginsburg
Gertrude Schaffner Goldberg

in consultation with
Ward Morehouse, Leonard Rodberg, Sumner Rosen,
June Zaccone

D1605653

NEW INITIATIVES FOR FULL EMPLOYMENT
c/o Council on International and Public Affairs
777 United Nations Plaza, Suite 3C
New York, NY 10017
1994

Published by The Apex Press, an imprint of the Council on International and Public Affairs, Suite 3C, 777 United Nations Plaza, New York, NY 10017 (Tel: 212/972-9877; Fax: 212/972-9878)

ISBN 0-945257-55-4

Cover design by Alan Goldberg

Typeset and printed in the United States of America

TABLE OF CONTENTS

ACKNOWLEDGEMENTS

This document is the work of many people who have dedicated long hours to discussing the concepts and policies employed, and providing critical feedback. In addition to the major contributors, we wish to acknowledge the invaluable contributions of Sylvia Aron, John Atlee, Frank Bonilla, Keith Brooks, Dave Brown, Hector Cordero-Guzman, Peggy Crane, Robert Engler, David Gil, Nat Ginsburg, Philip Harvey, Nat Mills, Frank Riessman, Ruth Spitz, and Irving Weinstein. We especially want to thank Nat Mills for his computer services. We are also grateful to Robert Heilbroner, of the New School for Social Research, Ann Fagan Ginger of the Meicklejohn Civil Liberties Institute, Jörg Huffschmid of the University of Bremen, and members of Americans for Democratic Action and the Economic Policy Institute for their thoughtful critiques and suggestions. Social Policy and the Columbia University Seminar on Full Employment have, over the years, provided us with a forum for presenting research and testing ideas.

SUMMARY

. . . being out of work, he was, as a consequence, out of temper with the world, and society, and his nearest kin.

Thomas Hardy, *The Mayor of Casterbridge*

Why Full Employment?

JOBS FOR ALL is a comprehensive program to ensure suitable jobs at good wages for everyone who wants to work. It emerges from the recognition that our current system of production and exchange is failing millions of people, both domestically and globally. It is based on the philosophy that work and production, exchange and distribution should be redesigned in ways that are conducive to the full development of the innate potential of all people and to the sustainability of the ecosystem.

Full employment is both an ethical imperative and the key to economic justice and prosperity. It is critical in securing those civil and political rights that are the bedrock of American democracy. People who are denied their right to a job cannot participate effectively as citizens in political life. We must reject the cruel contradiction between the rhetoric of the "work ethic" and the denial of jobs to millions.

In recent decades, callous indifference to unemployment has been exacerbated by widespread acceptance in some circles of the idea of a so-called "natural" rate of unemployment. Proponents often mislead-ingly call this rate—which they claim is from 6 to 7 percent—"full employment." They warn that efforts to push joblessness below this level would set off accelerating inflation. Professor William Vickrey, in his 1993 presidential address to the American Economics Association, tagged this so-called natural rate of unemployment "one of the most vicious euphemisms ever coined." But fiscal and monetary policies have often been directed toward maintaining this "natural" rate of unemployment and even toward increasing unemployment if it falls below its "natural" rate.

We reject the idea that unemployment is ever desirable and we reject the use of unemployment to fight inflation. Real full employment is feasible and achievable in the modern global economy. The key barriers are political and ideological, not just technical or economic. By demonstrating the feasibility of full employment, we hope to empower those who share our commitment to this priority.

Jobs for All: A Multi-issue Program

The members of New Initiatives for Full Employment (NIFE) who prepared this document understand that even the most coherent and persuasive program constitutes only the first step toward the political changes required to establish the national priority of full employment. Advocates have advanced a wide range of proposals on behalf of the unemployed, workers at risk from military cuts, racial/ethnic minorities, women, the disabled, older workers, immigrants and other disadvantaged groups. We believe that full employment is the necessary link among these different constituencies, providing a broad base for unified action and advocacy. In itself, full employment will not deal completely with the problems facing different groups, but we believe it is the necessary precondition for reducing the barriers to their resolution. Full employment also offers superior solutions to the problems of the deficit, poverty, homelessness, crime and other economic and social problems that paralyze our political process and harm our society.

An Idea With a History

There is nothing new about a full employment program. It was the centerpiece of Franklin Delano Roosevelt's "Economic Bill of Rights," proposed in 1944 as part of his last State of the Union Message. In it he called for jobs for everyone willing and able to work. The Universal

Declaration of Human Rights and the International Covenant on Economic, Social and Cultural Rights recognize work as a basic human right. However, domestic legislation, including the Employment Act of 1946 and the Humphrey-Hawkins Full Employment and Balanced Growth Act of 1978, has fallen far short of this goal. Our call for a new legislative commitment to full employment is put forward in the spirit of the Roosevelt heritage.

A Changed Employment Landscape

The global economy is one of many developments that has vastly transformed the economic landscape. It is even larger now that it encompasses all of Eastern Europe and the former Soviet Union. Multinational corporations are less accountable than ever to domestic governments or to the workers and communities whose livelihoods they can destroy. The 15 largest global corporations today have gross incomes greater than the gross domestic products (GDP) of over 120 countries and can play governments and workforces off against each other like pieces on a giant chess board.

The accelerated pace of computerized production and operations which shrink jobs and undermine workers' skills is another part of the changing employment landscape. Caught between the demands of family and a workplace that remains unresponsive to family needs, women are a major and growing share of the changing world economy. The pressure on ecological limits raises the imperative of sustainable development for the globe itself. All these changes in the employment landscape pose problems of understanding and policy, but we do not see them as incompatible with a comprehensive strategy that embraces both domestic and international policy measures.

The Prospects for Full Employment

Clearly JOBS FOR ALL cannot be implemented overnight. A frank acknowledgement of the barriers to a full employment strategy is a precondition of its political effectiveness. We see no reason why we cannot move rapidly toward authentic full employment over a two to three year period. The widening ranks of those who have been hurt by the job erosion of the recent past, and of those who are employed but at risk of job loss, improve the prospects for an effective political mobilization in support of full employment. We envisage a broad base of support among those who are hurt or at risk from increased inequality in the distribution of income and wealth, uncontrolled and unaccountable capital mobility, ever increasing and ever deeper poverty, barriers in job markets to blacks and other minorities, weakened ability of workers to organize into unions to protect their rights and negotiate better standards, and other forces destructive of economic well-being and dangerous to social stability.

In his presidential address to the American Economic Association, William Vickrey pointed out that there is no reason inherent in the real resources available to us why we cannot move—and rapidly— within two or three years to a situation of genuine full employment, estimated by Vickrey to be about 1.5 percent unemployment. We could then, according to Vickrey, continue indefinitely at that level and would enjoy a major reduction in poverty, homelessness, sickness and crime. We might also, he adds, see less resistance to reductions in military expenditures, to liberalization of trade and immigration policy, and to environmental protection programs. "We simply cannot," he told the nation's economists, "carry on as we have been doing without falling apart as a community and losing what is left of our status of world leadership."

Program and Principles

In the body of this document we have developed a plan and policies which are oriented around 11 principles. Each of these policies is suitable for Congressional action, but parallel action can also be taken at other levels, such as action by businesses, communities, and states. Together they would go far toward assuring all Americans the right to economic security and opportunity, and they would make a major contribution to international security. In brief, these are the principles.

1. JOBS FOR ALL: paid employment and phased reduction of work time without regard to race, gender, national origin, sexual preference, age or physical or mental disability. Certain forms of family care (e.g. of the very young and the infirm) should be recognized as productive work and should be compensated through paid family leave.

2. ADEQUATE INCOME FOR ALL: individual and family income sufficient for the full realization of human potential, to be acquired from paid employment, income

support, or a combination of the two.

3. RIGHTS OF WORKERS: to adequate compensation and benefits, to organize for their collective rights and interests, to job security during labor disputes, to training adequate to adapt to economic changes, to safe and healthy workplaces, to participation in decisions affecting their working life and security and to protection of wage and benefit standards for part-time and temporary workers.

4. COMMUNITY INVESTMENT, PRESERVATION AND SUPPORT: to ensure that enterprises are accountable to the communities where they operate for all decisions that affect the level of employment and the economic and ecological well-being of the community.

5. MILITARY CONVERSION: substantial and continuing reductions in military spending, with assurance that the "peace dividend" is committed to meeting the nation's large backlog of unmet social, physical, educational and infrastructure needs, and that those at risk of job loss be fully protected and actively helped in the transition from the military economy to useful civilian work.

6. ENVIRONMENTAL PRESERVATION AND SUSTAINABILITY: sustainable growth as the central principle in the restructuring of economic activity—both a necessity for survival, and beneficial to the economy and the people who work in it.

7. FAIR TRADE AND ECONOMICALLY VIABLE LOCAL PRODUCTION FOR LOCAL CONSUMPTION: government commitment to develop international standards ensuring that globalized production preserves and enhances, rather than undermines or destroys hard-won living standards, and that local autonomy and productive ability are protected.

8. DEMOCRATIC PLANNING AND INDUSTRIAL POLICY: democratic planning at all levels of government to ensure balance between private and public investment, and between private needs met through market mechanisms and public needs financed through equitable taxation.

9. REBUILDING THE NATION'S CITIES: reversing the deterioration of urban America, reducing urban-based poverty and homelessness, and restoring our neglected cities to their rightful place as the jewels of our civilization and engines of economic renewal.

10. SOUND GOVERNMENT FINANCE: moving from obsession with debt and deficits to creative use of fiscal and monetary instruments to promote economic stabilization and renewal, through a more progressive tax structure, a level of taxation adequate to meet national needs, fiscal balance at the real full employment level, and large-scale public investment to reduce our social, environmental, human capital and other accumulated, damaging deficits.

11. LIFELONG LEARNING: access to free educational and training opportunities and support for workers displaced from declining industries, from industries undergoing changes in occupational structure, and for persons reentering the labor market following family care, to enable people to realize their potential, and to assure adaptation of the work force to rapid changes in the operations of the national and global economies.

We invite all who are committed to the struggle for economic justice to examine this plan, to provide us with your proposals for change or addition, to help us build the political base of support needed, and to participate with us in developing the legislative proposals and strategies needed to achieve jobs for all in a nation that works.

INTRODUCTION: THE

"SILENT DEPRESSION"

In spite of what leading economic indicators say, America is in deep trouble. Yvonne Harris, a former office manager and bookkeeper, is one of millions caught in this trouble. Waiting on line with hundreds of other jobless workers at a State Department of Labor Office in New York City in February 1994, it was little consolation to her that many of the nation's economic indicators were pointing to an end to the recession. For, as she told a *New York Times* reporter, she had gone from "being a Cinderella to a Raggedy Ann: I've worked my whole life, and now this."

There are other signs of this deep trouble. In our decaying central cities, where an entire generation of young people is growing up without any stake in production, men and women sleep under bridges and over heating grates in winter, children kill each other over a pair of sneakers or a wristwatch and bear babies addicted to crack/cocaine. In the Northeast, the Mid-Atlantic and Midwest, displaced industrial workers earn one-third to one-half of their former pay in a service sector that is, itself, now exporting jobs. Around the country displaced middle managers collect unemployment insurance and watch their life savings go down the drain, while recent college graduates punch icons on a cash register or sit in secretarial pools, despairing of the "good jobs" their higher education once promised. In California, the children of those who flocked to the land of sunshine seeking a better life find many libraries locked, the elementary school year foreshortened, and the

15

public colleges to which they have aspired facing program cuts and
overcrowded classrooms. In the ports of entry for new immigrants,
sweatshops and child labor abound; and even in the South, which in
recent years boasted the fastest growth of any region, workers' wages
remain low and the region is still the poorest in the nation.

Nearly 37 million (over one in seven) Americans lived below the
"official" poverty line in 1992, including over one in four Hispanics,
and over one in three African Americans. Over one in five children,
including nearly 40 percent of Hispanic children and nearly half of all
African American children lived in poverty in 1992. Many of those
counted as poor are either employed persons or their dependents.
Moreover, because the official poverty standard is a paltry one, many
people with incomes above the poverty line cannot afford the basic
necessities, especially adequate housing. Of the seven industrialized
nations whose poverty rates were compared in the Luxembourg Income
Study, the United States had the highest poverty rates for both single
parent families and all families with children. For single parent families
the U.S. rate was more than twice the rate of Germany and over three
times that of France. For all families with children, the U.S. rate was 40
percent greater than that of the United Kingdom, the country with the
next highest rate of poverty.

These are but a few of the symptoms of what economist Wallace
Peterson has called the "silent depression." It is "silent" because it
measures a longer and slower growing decline in real (adjusted for
inflation) incomes, rather than the shorter fluctuations of traditional
economic indicators like the GDP and even the official unemployment
rate. Policymakers, relying on these traditional measures, have thus
failed to come to grips with the economic crisis faced by millions of
Americans. The public, however, is cognizant of this silent depression,
even if the policymakers refuse to recognize it. It is reflected in
numerous public opinion polls that have detected a shift in attitudes
from confidence about the future to frustration and resignation over the
realization that the generation starting out today will be unable to do
better than its parents.

Peterson locates the start of this "silent depression" in 1973, when
the rate of growth of two key indicators of economic well-being, the
real income of the average worker and *real* median family income,
began to decline. By 1990, the *real* income of the average worker was
19.1 percent below the level of 1973. Since 1973, *real* family incomes
for married couples with heads between the ages of 35 and 64 have
grown much more slowly than in previous years, but for younger

families they have actually declined. This, in spite of the fact that the family now sends more members into the work force than it did prior to 1973!

Another indicator of the "silent depression" is the rising rate of unemployment. Though economic growth has begun to pick up after the most recent recession, the official unemployment rate has continued to hover above six percent. The longer trend, however, is even more telling. The rate of unemployment, even at the height of each succeeding business cycle (when unemployment is supposed to decline), has been steadily increasing since 1973 and along with it, the standard of unemployment found acceptable to policymakers. Even this standard underestimates, by more than half, the number of real jobless (see Section 1, "Jobs for All").

More than cash income is at stake, however. Thirty-nine million people lack basic health care. Millions more have inadequate coverage and could be devastated by a major illness. Nearly 27 million (more than one in ten) Americans are on food stamps, a higher proportion than at any time since the program began.

Moreover, the gap between the rich and poor and between the average worker and the chief executive officer (CEO)—telling indicators of economic fairness—have grown wider since 1979, reversing the post-war trend toward greater equality. In 1992, the poorest fifth of American families received only 4.4 percent of all family income, while the top 20 percent of American families received 44.6 percent and the top 5 percent received 17.6 percent (more than the poorest 40 percent!). During the 1980s, the income of the top 1 percent grew by 63 percent, capturing more than half of total income growth among families. The CEO in major corporations in the United States made 26 times as much as the average production worker in 1992, compared with 10.6 times as much in Germany and 11.4 times as much in Japan. Such figures make the economic polarization in the United States among the most extreme in the industrialized world.

Another measure of national well-being is the "Index of Social Health," developed by Fordham University's Institute for Innovation in Social Policy. This index is a composite of 16 social and economic indicators collected by the Census Bureau, such as infant mortality, child abuse, drug abuse, unemployment and high school drop-out rates. According to the Institute's 1993 report, America's social health has declined more than 50 percent since 1970.

In addition to economic stagnation and growing social pathologies, the nation witnessed a decade of greed and economic mismanagement in the 1980s. In the public sector tremendous increases in the federal deficit and debt (which stems from accumulated deficits) are some of the legacies of that era. While much of the industrialized world is also caught in a general economic slowdown and many nations also have large deficits and debts, some features of the U.S. situation are noteworthy. For example, much of the debt was acquired during those years with huge tax cuts and tremendous increases in the military budget. So it was the result of wasteful, or counterproductive measures, rather than of policies designed to meet the human and infrastructure needs of the American people.

These conditions call for bold and courageous leadership and innovative policies. At present, however, the political agenda appears to have been captured by an economic oligarchy. These are the people who benefited most from the speculation and mismanagement of the 1980s, who are now reaping the benefits of the government's fixation on the deficit, and who are largely untouched by the "silent depression."

Yet, there is hope. All over the country, millions of people in community and single-issue organizations, even in the poorest communities, are struggling to make a better life for themselves and their neighbors, and thousands of others meet in small self-help groups to offer each other fellowship and mutual aid. These as yet unorganized, unpoliticized and disunited groups form the nucleus of what could be a new people's movement for economic democracy.

The program outlined in these pages seeks to expand the debate about what is needed to meet the deep longing of the majority of Americans for meaningful work and economic security. We believe the failure of our national leaders to commit themselves to a full employment policy lies at the heart of our nation's economic malaise, and we have proposed a program for full employment as a necessary, though not sufficient, condition for its resolution. Many of the programs presented here have been proposed by a variety of groups, and some have even been introduced by the President or members of Congress. However, most of them have been proposed in piecemeal fashion—as responses to specific concerns of single-issue or constituency groups, or as cures for some symptom of the general problem.

In his thorough study of employment policy since World War II, Gary Mucciaroni cites as one reason for the lack of constituent support for full employment the government's orientation toward providing programs for the relief of the temporarily unemployed rather than a comprehensive commitment to meeting the economic needs of the entire nation. Mucciaroni also believes that the lack of a full employment policy robbed other proposals of a coherence and overarching purpose.

By demonstrating that full employment is tied to the solutions of other problems—such as the budget deficit, poverty, homelessness, crime, family stress, decaying infrastructure and environmental degradation—that is, by making it do more than just give jobs to the jobless, we increase its potential constituency.

The writers of this document recognize that we live in a vastly transformed and intricately interrelated economic and political landscape: a global economy that is no longer accountable either to national governments or to the workers and communities that make it possible; a productive power now so automated that it is rendering obsolete more and more sectors of our workforce and the skills that once made their labor remunerative; a national labor market increasingly characterized by contingent work; a world in which conflicts, both domestic and international, often stem from the disparity between those with remunerative jobs and those without; a workplace in which most women are now a permanent part and which, therefore, must be more responsive to family needs; and finally, an economy which is running up against global ecological limits, vastly slowed growth, and burgeoning debt, even in the wealthiest of nations.

We recognize that JOBS FOR ALL cannot be implemented overnight. However, the proposals presented in these pages point in the direction we must move if this nation is to fulfill its historic destiny as a noble experiment in democracy. It is time to move away from our current role as the world's military superpower, feared by all, toward that of a powerful example of economic and social justice to be emulated by all. With abundant resources, wisely managed, and with the diversity of our people seen as a strength rather than a weakness, we can be both prosperous and generous.

We invite all those who are engaged in the struggle for economic justice and a safe and secure environment to examine this program, to consider the political strategies that we propose in its final pages, and to join us in developing the legislative initiatives and political pressure necessary for its achievement.

JOBS FOR ALL: THE GREAT UNFINISHED TASK OF AMERICAN DEMOCRACY

We believe that jobs at decent wages for all who seek employment are the keys to democratic justice and economic recovery. Not only is full employment an ethical imperative. It is also critical to securing those civil and political rights that are the bedrock of American democracy. In a nation that seems to prefer employment to government transfers as the major source of economic security, it is a cruel irony to emphasize the work ethic and then deny people the ability to exercise it. While there is no formal property requirement for political participation or the enjoyment of civil liberties, people with limited incomes neither enjoy the full protection of their civil liberties and rights, nor are they able to participate effectively in political life. Furthermore, their ability to fulfill their social roles in the family and community is stunted. A fully employed people is thus the linchpin of a viable modern democracy.

Full employment is also key to preserving our increasingly fragile ecosystem. Only through the economic security provided by thoughtfully planned full employment can we resist the lure of employment that is destructive of the environment or the poverty conditions that are also leading to its degradation.

Full employment is also critical for peace, both domestic and international. Unemployment is a crime, robbing people of the chance to be productive members of their society. It often fosters among those who are denied productive dignity resentment and rage, which can erupt in racism and nativism. During the Second World War, President Roosevelt observed that "necessitous men are not free men. People who are hungry and out of a job are the stuff of which dictatorships are made." Though human conflict is not determined solely by economic distress, neither domestic tranquility nor international peace can be achieved without the economic security provided by full employment.

Securing the Right to Employment

Full employment is not a new proposal. It has been the rallying cry of numerous social movements from the middle of the nineteenth century on. But in 1944 this concept was articulated by the highest authority in the land. In his State of the Union message, President Roosevelt proposed the adoption of an "Economic Bill of Rights" which, among other economic rights, called for the guarantee of a job for everyone willing and able to work.

Subsequent to Roosevelt's call for economic rights, several international agreements recognized work as a basic human right. The United Nations Charter (Article 55) binds member states to "promote . . . full employment," which at the time was clearly understood as a mandate to ensure remunerative work for all job seekers. The Charter is a treaty ratified after a Senate vote of 89-2 and part of the "supreme law of the land" under the U.S. Constitution. Article 23 of the Universal Declaration of Human Rights, adopted by member states in 1948, gives further substantive content to work as a human right, stating that "everyone has the right to work, to free choice of employment, to just and favorable conditions of work," to "protection against unemployment," to "equal pay for equal work," and to "just and favorable remuneration ensuring . . . an existence worthy of human dignity." The International Covenant on Economic, Social and Cultural Rights goes even further in defining economic rights. President Carter signed this Covenant in 1977; it has been awaiting Senate ratification ever since.

Even though the Universal Declaration of Human Rights is not a treaty and therefore does not bind signatories to legally enforceable obligations, it is an important articulation of the nature of the human rights goals that members of the United Nations are obliged to promote under the terms of the Charter. The Covenant on Economic, Social and Cultural Rights, even before ratification, has a significant legal status. The Declaration and the Covenant, by virtue of their widespread acceptance, have assumed an independent status as statements of customary international law. Irrespective of their recognition by governments, however, we believe the rights proclaimed in such documents are basic to human dignity and development. Slavery violated the human rights of slaves, whether or not the law recognized the violation. We believe the same is true of hunger, involuntary unemployment, and other violations of rights proclaimed in the Universal Declaration and International Covenant.

In the United States, Bertram Gross, a long-time proponent of the right to employment and a central figure in the two major struggles to secure this right through legislation, has criticized its erosion in the watered-down laws that eventually passed: The Employment Act of 1946 and the Full Employment and Balanced Growth Act of 1978. Despite their weaknesses, both could have been used by our government to move toward full employment, but neither was ever adequately implemented and the mandate of the latter has been consistently violated. Recently, in *Securing the Right to Employment*, economist and lawyer Philip Harvey has argued that opponents of government initiatives for the jobless are almost never asked to justify their position in human rights terms. Harvey believes that the existence of such a powerful human rights claim could, and should, be used to galvanize support for a jobs-for-all movement, to demoralize the opposition and to alter the terms of debate over government goals.

Obstacles to a Full Employment at Decent Wages Strategy

Critical to implementing a full employment strategy is frank recognition of the obstacles to such a strategy and genuine commitment to overcoming them.

One such obstacle is the increasing concentration of economic and political power in corporate hands. Declining real wages of industrial workers (now lower than they were in 1973) is one manifestation of this power. Another manifestation is the proliferation of poverty-level jobs that has pushed more Americans below the government's unrealistically low poverty line than at any time in the past 20 years. Still another is the loss of power of American workers, which is evidenced by their declining rate of unionization. At less than 16 percent (11.5 percent in the private sector) this rate of unionization is lower than in most other major industrialized countries. More extensive unionization has not prevented high unemployment in many Western European nations. However, it has kept wage erosion, despite intercountry differences, as yet relatively modest (with the exception of Great Britain) and there is generally much better income protection for the jobless.

We urgently need new mechanisms to hold corporations truly accountable to those most directly affected by their actions—namely, their workers, consumers, and the communities in which they have major facilities. It will require real effort to overcome the juggernaut of corporate power, but we will never have decent jobs for all unless it is done. We address these issues in JOBS FOR ALL (see Section 2, "Adequate Income," Section 3, "Rights of Workers," Section 4, "Community Investment, Preservation and Support," Section 6, "Environmental Preservation and Sustainability," and Section 7, "Fair Trade and Economically Viable Local Production for Local Consumption").

A second obstacle to achieving full employment is what John Kenneth Galbraith has recently called the "culture of contentment." Galbraith claims that for the first time, we have a well-off voting majority. Contented with their situation, they oppose any improvement in the conditions of the poor, exercising power by endorsing only those policies that serve their narrow pecuniary interests. Further, a bargain has been struck between the upper middle class and the rich. For fear of disturbing their own tax situation, the upper middle class does not support raising taxes on the rich. As we see it, this underscores the need for greater participation and influence by those who are less priviledged. The current tilt in Congress toward those sectors of our society that are most opposed to full employment reflects these conditions. While we do not address this issue, we recognize that campaign finance reform is a prior condition for overcoming the undue influence of those who would prevent Congress from doing the right thing.

A third obstacle to full employment is the increasing mobility of capital, leading to job loss and lower work and environmental standards. Some brakes on the unrestricted international movement of capital must be applied in order to assure greater corporate accountability to workers and communities, even though blanket restrictions on the international movement of capital are not the answer. We address these issues in JOBS FOR ALL (see Section 3, "Rights of Workers," Section 4, "Community Investment, Preservation and Support," Section 6, "Environmental Preservation and Sustainability," Section 7, "Fair Trade and Economically Viable Local Production for Local Consumption").

A fourth obstacle to full employment is the increasing tendency of business to replace full-time workers with temporary and part-time employees. It appears that about half the jobs people have been getting in the last few years are part-time or temporary, though federal figures are sketchy. While starting out in the service sector, this phenomenon has now spread to manufacturing. These "contingent" jobs (some call them "throwaway" or "disposable" jobs) are now so prevalent that the government no longer knows how many people actually work in American factories. Contingent jobs usually pay less than regular jobs and come with few, if any, benefits. Related to increased global competition, the growth of contingent work has to be seen as a systemic change in the structure of the labor market that, unless addressed by government policy, spells increasing hardship for workers and their families (see Section 1, "Jobs for All," Section 2, "Adequate Income for All," and Section 3, "Rights of Workers").

The rapidity with which automation is replacing human labor is the fifth obstacle to full employment. While automation could be used to relieve workers of tedious, repetitive and "dirty" jobs in order to free them for more creative work, it appears instead to be creating large numbers of surplus workers. Moreover, for many of those still employed, automation has not made life easier. Rather, the speed up of production appears to have added to job stress.

A sixth obstacle is the failure—abetted by official measures of unemployment—to recognize the full magnitude of economic distress. As Secretary of Labor, Robert Reich, noted in testimony at his confirmation hearing, the official unemployment rate is woefully inadequate as a measure of joblessness. The number of jobless would be more than twice as large if the statistically hidden jobless were included along with the officially jobless in the unemployment rate (see Section 1, "Jobs for All"). This means that in 1992, there may have been as many as 22 million fully or partially jobless people in the United States; a government economic stimulus package that was designed to yield 500,000 jobs—such as the Clinton Administration proposed—was a step so tentative that the President could not inspire the majority of the nation to rally to its support. We address this obstacle in JOBS FOR ALL (see Section 1, "Jobs for All").

A seventh barrier to full employment lies in the fact that what may be a social problem for the vast majority of the population is actually a benefit to an influential minority. Such is the "problem" of unemployment and underemployment. Although business leaders find euphemisms for talking about unemployment, such as the need to keep labor costs down, many clearly benefit from a slack labor market. Unemployment keeps wages down, renders workers more docile, easier to control and less likely to join unions. However, in the long run, unemployment and declining wages are not only bad for workers, but for the economy as a whole. Indeed, many businesses would also benefit from full employment through increased demand for their products and services. Ultimately, we all pay more for unemployment in increased costs for crime, disease, homelessness, welfare, environmental destruction and the like.

An eighth, and final obstacle to full employment, has to do with certain myths that continue to haunt our political culture. Ray Marshall, when he was Secretary of Labor, attributed much of the opposition and indifference to full employment to several persistent myths. One is the myth that unemployment is necessary to curb inflation. Another is that unemployment is not due to a lack of jobs, but to the unwillingness of the unemployed to work. Still a third myth recognized by Marshall is the assumption that we cannot create enough meaningful jobs.

We address each of these obstacles in JOBS FOR ALL.

It will not be easy to overcome the obstacles to full employment, but doing so will allow the United States to fulfill its promise to create a truly democratic society. We have moved a long way toward political democracy for all Americans, but we have fallen short in securing meaningful economic democracy. Obstacles to the achievement of full employment, however, are more political than technical. We will have to galvanize a massive social movement to exert the necessary political muscle to effect meaningful change.

Full Employment and Income Support

The overall goal of a full employment policy is the reduction of poverty and the achievement of economic justice. Though JOBS FOR ALL takes a giant step in this direction, it does not obviate the need for government income support. The costs of paying for necessities falls too much on the shoulders of individuals and families, and these costs must be shared by the state. The burdens for which government must assume more responsibility include:

Housing costs. For many people, rent or mortgage payments exceed the traditional 25 or 30 percent of income. This burden is especially hard on low-income workers, whose housing costs often reach or exceed half their incomes.

Medical care costs. These are especially burdensome for single parents, people who are unemployed, who work for small- or medium-sized enterprises or are self-employed. The lack of universal, tax-supported provision of medical care forces people either to forgo medical care or to work longer hours than is consistent with other family and social responsibilities in order to pay for medical care.

Education. Especially at the college level and beyond, education must be paid for out of private resources far more in the United States than in most comparably developed societies. The need to meet steadily rising costs of higher and professional education denies these opportunities to many Americans and distorts work-leisure choices for many others.

Care of children, disabled and infirm family members. Child care costs prevent many women from full participation in the labor force. Care of seniors is especially hard on the aging children of the frail elderly, particularly their daughters. The parents and/or siblings of the mentally and physically disabled confront similar dilemmas.

For growing numbers of all social classes, the earlier promise of economic affluence has been transformed into inescapable pressures to earn enough to meet burdens which should be borne by government and paid for from taxes levied equitably on all groups. When government assumes appropriate responsibility for these necessities, it will also be creating employment opportunities for many whose productive capacities are now wasted.

THE PROGRAM: PRINCIPLES AND STRATEGIES

The program that follows is premised on a set of 11 principles that guide the adoption of specific strategies, each of which is elaborated in some detail in the main body of the book. Each strategy is designed to lead to the development of specific pieces of legislation that could be enacted by Congress. Together, such legislation would go a long way toward assuring every person in the United States the right to economic security and would also contribute to the economic security of people in other nations.

The 11 principles in this document focus primarily on jobs for all. They do not focus on government responsibility for the essential goods and services to which we have already alluded, such as medical care, shelter or the need for major changes in our public school system to prepare young people for the new labor market. Programs to provide these essentials must be addressed separately. We firmly believe the state should ease the burden of the costs of these necessities for all citizens.

Adoption of a national health insurance program would make care universal and would relieve some of the employment barriers that stem from the high costs of employer-provided insurance. And, employment levels in the health care field would eventually rise if we meet our needs for health care more adequately. With jobs at decent wages, people will be in a better position to pay for housing; but the shortage of affordable housing and the high proportions of total income that many are obliged to spend on shelter must be addressed separately from jobs and wages, perhaps through new entitlement programs. The targeting of some jobs programs for housing (see Section 9, "Rebuilding the Nation's Cities"), would, of course, contribute both to job creation and shelter rights. While we address the need for lifelong learning and propose education and training programs for adult and young adult workers and displaced homemakers, we believe the more fundamental problems of the educational system that must be met before the potential worker reaches adulthood are being addressed by others with more competence in the field.

THE PLAN IN BRIEF:

PRINCIPLES AND STRATEGIES

1. JOBS FOR ALL

All people—regardless of race, gender, national origin, sexual preference, physical disability, age or previous incarceration—shall have the opportunity for decently paid employment. Vital family work shall also be recognized as a contribution to the nation's economy.

Strategies:

1.1 Establishment of a high-level government Commission to Study and Propose Solutions to the Problem of Unemployment and Underemployment in order to contribute to public recognition of the problem and to support a more vigorous effort to expand employment opportunity. Subcommittees of the Commission to study and make recommendations for programs to help groups and regions with special needs, such as the rural poor, displaced or endangered family farmers, farmworkers, Appalachians and Native Americans.

1.2 In addition to the official unemployment rate, equal prominence to be given to a newly developed measure of unemployment that includes *all* persons without employment who want to work and *all* involuntary part-time workers who want more hours of work. In addition, a composite sub-employment index that includes those employed at poverty wages to be developed.

1.3 Macroeconomic policies to stimulate job creation in the market economy and reduce the deficit, including low real interest rates and vigorous public investment, a measure which has been shown to yield substantial growth in GDP.

1.4 Standby government job creation, initially for half of the officially unemployed, with the eventual goal of complete coverage of the nation's jobless. Emphasis on jobs that are environmentally sustainable and socially useful and that contribute to economic growth through public investment.

1.5 Increased federal support for the arts, including the establishment of a national theater, to meet the need for quality and accessibility in our cultural life, to encourage new and aspiring talent, and to provide employment for unemployed artists, writers and performers.

1.6 Staged reductions in standard work time, including both a reduced work week and legally mandated paid vacations, sabbaticals and work sharing, in order to stimulate job creation and afford more time for family, community, leisure and learning. These are especially vital for many parents of young children and for many disabled and older workers.

1.7 Creation of disincentives for using overtime (hence, the creation of new jobs) by raising the legal rate of overtime pay and by levying all employer payroll taxes on all overtime earnings, even if the worker's income already exceeds the maximum taxable earnings.

1.8 Legislative protection of wage and benefit standards for part-time workers.

1.9 Encouragement of tripartite cooperation among business, labor and government to prevent inflation.

1.10 Tax and labor market policies to curb inflation, if the need arises, such as: research on how many jobs are actually vacant, where they are located and what skills they actually require; extensive labor market training programs; a national computerized employment service with mandatory job listings; mobility grants for jobless workers; controls on prices, profits, executive salaries, professional fees, wages and the like. Controls, if deemed necessary, should be equitably applied, so as not to harm those with modest incomes.

1.11 Enforcement of existing anti-discrimination laws and affirmative action programs and the enactment of new legislation to achieve pay equity and equitable distribution of jobs and economic rewards, particularly among groups which have suffered discrimination based on race, gender, national origin, sexual orientation, disability or age, or those who have suffered sexual harassment.

1.12 A special unit in the Department of Labor to be created to coordinate the efforts of government, private sector and community-based organizations to disseminate job and training information and to achieve an appropriate match between individuals and jobs.

1.13 Acceptance of and adherence to international standards for full employment and economic justice, such as the International Labour Organization's conventions on child labor, the rights of unions and workplace health and safety, as well as ratification of the United Nations' International Covenant for Economic, Social and Cultural Rights. These are ways of bringing the United States into compliance with internationally agreed upon norms for full employment and economic justice and would contribute toward the advancement of a global "New Deal."

1.14 A global employment summit to be convened by the United Nations to discuss barriers to and create the mechanisms for moving toward global full employment within a framework of environmentally sustainable development.

2. ADEQUATE INCOME FOR ALL

All people shall have an income sufficient for the full development of their human potential, whether from wage employment, income support or a combination of the two.

Strategies:

2.1 An increase in the minimum wage with the immediate goal of an income for one worker that is equivalent to the current poverty level for a family of four, the end goal being the indexing of the minimum wage to a revised poverty standard.

2.2 An upward revision of the poverty standard to reflect actual needs as well as regional differences in costs of living.

2.3 Provision of paid family leaves at an adequate replacement rate (with a goal of up to two years) for family members who interrupt their employment and earnings to provide care in the home to the very young and infirm. Benefits to be treated as part of taxable household income.

2.4 Expanded opportunities for job training and education for family care givers, in order to minimize losses in occupational development and mobility as a result of absence from the labor market.

2.5 Universal, quality subsidized child care to be available to pre-school age children beginning at the age of two. Benefits to be treated as part of taxable household income.

2.6 Government-guaranteed child support for all single-parent families, to be treated as part of taxable income.

2.7 Monthly child allowances for all children, to be treated as part of taxable income.

2.8 Strengthening of the unemployment insurance program by: extending benefits to *all* wage and salary workers, including contingent workers, as well as reentrants to the labor force; increasing benefit levels to provide meaningful income support; extending benefits to 65 weeks, and longer for older workers; and coupling them to government-provided health benefits and to a government standby jobs program, so that workers who exhaust their benefits without finding a job in the private sector are not left without either a job or health care.

2.9 Strengthening of the national Disability Insurance program and expansion of state Workers' Compensation programs. The establishment of a new national program to cover temporary, non-work-connected disability, including maternity.

3. RIGHTS OF WORKERS

All workers, including contingent workers, have the right to decent compensation and occupational benefits as well as the right to organize for their collective well-being and the right to job security during labor disputes. Workers' rights also include safe workplaces and meaningful participation in workplace decision-making.

Strategies:

3.1 Passage of legislation to restore the original intent of the Wagner National Labor Relations Act of 1935 by assuring workers the exclusive and uncoerced right to decide whether to join and be represented by a union.

3.2 New legislation barring employers from permanently replacing striking workers.

3.3 Revision of the Fair Labor Standards Act to restore one of its original aims, which was to encourage employers to hire new workers.

3.4 New legislation to protect contingent workers, such as guaranteed hourly wage parity among all workers doing the same job, pro-rated fringe benefits, and protection of other work-related rights.

3.5 New legislation to protect the rights of workers to their earned fringe benefits in retirement.

3.6 Increased funding to upgrade the government agencies responsible for protecting health and safety at work, as well as better and larger staffs, and greater power to assess and improve health and safety hazards.

3.7 New legislation to assure all workers freedom of information concerning threats to occupational health and safety, as well as access to impartial government adjudication of health and safety claims.

3.8 New legislation that assures workers the right to participate in decisions regarding the number, quality, geographic location and content of their jobs and access to the information relevant to these decisions.

3.9 Recognition of the cultural diversity of the current and future workforce through legislation that protects workers' language and cultural rights, as well as adequate support to encourage and enable immigrants to learn English.

3.10 New legislation to extend full protection of all labor statutes and all provisions of negotiated contracts to undocumented workers.

4. COMMUNITY INVESTMENT, PRESERVATION AND SUPPORT

The nation and its communities shall have access to the resources generated by the labor of its citizens.

Strategies:

4.1 A "stay or pay" policy to restrict the right of capital to desert communities and evade U.S. labor and environmental laws without compensating the workers and communities they leave behind.

4.2 An end to the foreign tax credit and tax deferral privileges through which the United States tax code encourages U.S.-based multinationals to transfer jobs abroad rather than keeping them at home. Strict enforcement of the law barring USAID support for investment promotion programs that lure U.S. businesses to relocate in low-wage countries.

4.3 A system of local, regional and national public investment banks to channel credit in ways that support productive investment in local community development and environmental preservation and that counter financial instability.

4.4 Democratic planning processes, starting at the local level, based upon the principle of "community federalism." These would plan for local job creation and placement, prepare inventories of local needs, and prepare for increased local provision of goods and services (where feasible). They would also plan for environmental protection, affirmative action, preservation of stable communities, and the creation of humane work environments (see 8.1, 8.2).

5. MILITARY CONVERSION

Substantial cuts shall be made in military spending, with the peace dividend being used primarily to meet the nation's vast social and economic needs and to aid displaced members of the armed forces and defense workers in transferring to civilian employment.

Strategies:

5.1 Substantial cuts in military spending on the order of the Congressional Black Caucus' proposal for halving the military budget within four years.

5.2 Adoption of a national conversion plan that would educate and train displaced defense workers for new jobs in the civilian economy, provide transitional income support, assist businesses and communities in converting to civilian production, and assist industries serving military bases to convert to new markets. A National Office of Economic Conversion should be established to develop and implement such a plan in consultation with local community and plant-based "alternative use" committees.

5.3 Priority in the use of the peace dividend to meeting human needs and financing environmentally safe energy and mass transit systems.

5.4 Stronger measures to develop international agreements to halt the arms trade, enforcement of the Nuclear Non-proliferation Treaty Implementation Act and ratification of all pending treaties to cut nuclear and conventional weaponry.

6. ENVIRONMENTAL PRESERVATION AND SUSTAINABILITY

The economic future of the nation, the health of human beings and the sustainability of life on earth demand that patterns of production and consumption be compatible with sustaining and regenerating the environment.

Strategies:

6.1 Priorities in job creation programs given to work that contributes to environmental conservation, cleanup, the development of renewable energy sources and to other non-polluting work such as human services.

6.2 Government policies (including regulation, subsidies, procurement and tax incentives) to encourage environmentally sustainable production processes and products, to establish a new industrial sector responsible for the recycling and reuse of secondary materials, to develop and use renewable, non-polluting energy sources, and to encourage climate stabilization.

6.3 Development of a new social and environmental accounting process to guide the nation's tax and spending policies.

6.4 Allocation of a greater percentage of federal research and development funds for the development of environmentally sustainable industry.

6.5 Comprehensive conversion programs for workers and communities negatively affected by the transition to an environmentally sustainable economy.

7. FAIR TRADE AND ECONOMICALLY VIABLE LOCAL PRODUCTION FOR LOCAL CONSUMPTION

Upward harmonization of global living standards, protection of workers' rights, environmental preservation, and the principle of local production for local consumption, where appropriate, shall be priorities in all trade agreements, private industry incentives, guarantees and tax concessions. U.S. financial support for international financial institutions shall be contingent on adherence to these principles.

Strategies:

7.1 International rules to govern the operation and movement of multinational corporations so they canot use their considerable bargaining power to negotiate concessions from poor countries as a condition for their investment.

7.2 Current and pending trade agreements to be reevaluated and renegotiated on the basis of maximum protection for workers and the environment, as well as greater emphasis on non-exploitative exchange relations, democratic decision-making, and, where feasible, local production for local consumption both in the United States and in the countries with which we trade.

7.3 Debt relief for poorer countries and other policies designed to promote upward harmonization of living standards within and among nations.

7.4 U.S. financial support for international financial agencies like the International Monetary Fund and the World Bank to be conditioned on their support for the principles of workers' rights, environmental protection, local production for local consumption, and enhancement of the quality of life for *all* people.

7.5 Incentives such as loan guarantees and tax concessions

to private industry to be conditioned on their guarantee of workers' rights, environmental safety, and local community empowerment and development both in the United States and abroad.

7.6 Support for generous transitional asistance to workers, industries and communities negatively impacted by international agreements and the globalization of production.

8. DEMOCRATIC PLANNING AND INDUSTRIAL POLICY

A commitment to full employment requires coordination of public and private economic policy for implementing this new social compact, including the development of a sound industrial policy for the nation.

Strategies:

8.1 Creation of a National Economic Coordinating Council to plan, develop and implement a national industrial policy. The Council to be composed of representatives of business, labor, the government and the general public.

8.2 Creation of local and regional Coordinating Councils to inform the National Economic Coordinating Council, plan for and allocate investment in local and regional projects and industries.

8.3 Creation of a sound industrial policy to integrate national economic policies and to coordinate federal, state and local tax and spending policies, national trade policies and education and training policies and to assure a healthy mix of manufacturing and services.

8.4 Creation of a National Civilian Technology Administration to stimulate investment in civilian technologies for mass transit systems, renewable energy production, climate stabilization, communications networks and the like.

8.5 Creation of an Industrial Extension Service to provide education and technical assistance to businesses which need to modernize or find new product lines in order to create or preserve secure, well-paid jobs.

9. REBUILDING THE NATION'S CITIES

A program targeted to the core poverty areas of our 100 largest cities that would help to rebuild both their badly deteriorated human and physical resources and contribute to the economic health of the nation.

Strategies

9.1 At least $50 billion a year to be spent on education, training, job creation, housing, mass transit, and support of small enterprise in our poorest urban areas.

9.2 A National Task Force to Rebuild the Nation's Cities to be established under the National Economic Coordinating Council and assigned the task of developing an integrated urban strategy, setting priorities, and monitoring the implementation of the program.

9.3 Development of a Civilian Youth Conservation Corps targeted at unemployed inner-city and rural youth, providing basic education, job training, life skills, drug rehabilitation, community renovation and job placement.

9.4 A priority to be placed on the development and rehabilitation of low-income housing in the inner cities, linking job creation with affordable housing. Support of the Jesse Gray Housing Bill of 1993 (H.R. 1380) as a means to this end.

9.5 Support for a shift in the health delivery system toward greater emphasis on health protection and promotion, with services decentralized at the community level. Assistance provided to workers who may be displaced in the transition to a new health care system.

10. SOUND GOVERNMENT FINANCE

The U.S. government shall adopt a fiscal policy that balances revenues with the expenditures necessary for economic and social revitalization in a full employment economy.

Strategies:

10.1 The federal deficit to be reduced by making the income tax more progressive, restoring the rates of non-Social Security receipts to proportions found acceptable through the mid-1970s.

10.2 Reduction of the federal deficit through the setting of unemployment reduction goals. Requiring Federal Reserve policy to also adhere to these goals.

10.3 Targeted tax credits for capital expenditures that would contribute to environmentally sustainable growth and job creation.

10.4 Reform of government accounting procedures to recognize the difference between "consumption" expenditures and "investment" expenditures, that is, those expenditures that in the long run contribute to economic growth and therefore to the public treasury.

11. LIFELONG LEARNING

Displaced workers and displaced homemakers shall have the opportunity for education to ease workforce transitions and to enable them to reach their full human potential.

Strategies:

11.1 Greater federal and business support for training and retraining programs to be linked to jobs and new job creation, and to include expansion of the apprenticeship training model beyond its traditional U.S. focus on the building and metal trades.

11.2 Enactment of a New Careers for Working Americans program that provides income and tuition support for workers displaced from industries that are declining or undergoing occupational shifts and for displaced homemakers entering or reentering the labor market at designated institutions of their choice. Such a program to provide job counseling and career relocation services before, during and at the completion of the program.

11.3 Affording workers the choice of converting productivity gains into partially compensated sabbaticals to enhance job-related skills or engage in personal enrichment.

THE PLAN IN FULL

1.

JOBS FOR ALL

A nation with sufficient resources and a commitment to human rights for all its people must either provide opportunities for them to earn a decent living, some form of income transfer, or a combination of the two. Official American rhetoric has been to prefer work to welfare. There are compelling reasons for a nation to choose employment over income support. M. Harvey Brenner and others have documented consistent correlations between rises in unemployment and increases in cardiovascular diseases, mental illnesses and even mortality rates. Other studies have shown rising unemployment associated with increases in social problems, such as substance abuse, family violence, and crime. The waste of human potential, the loss of both production and tax revenues, and the cost of unemployment insurance and remedial measures are further compelling reasons to support full employment.

Yet despite these compelling reasons, and its own rhetoric, the United States fails to provide sufficient opportunities for employment, living wages for many who do work, or adequate income support to persons of working age (many of them mothers) who have neither jobs nor sufficient income. Actual U.S. policy has been to provide insufficient work and inadequate welfare and to count on the "free market" to correct any imbalance between labor supply and demand over the long run.

Welfare "reform" in the 1980s exemplified these multiple binds for the poor. Many poor mothers were forced to enter a labor market characterized by chronic unemployment and underemployment, thereby expanding the low-wage labor pool and depressing wages still further.

The nation's failure to provide either employment at decent pay or adequate income transfers to all its people is attested to by the size of its poverty population, which was nearly 37 million in 1992. According to the Luxembourg Income Studies, the U.S. poverty rate for non-aged households, if measured as household income that falls below one-half the nation's adjusted median income, was more than twice that of Sweden and West Germany, nearly double that of France, and 45 percent higher than that of the United Kingdom.

Demonstrating a Federal Commitment to Full Employment

Given the myriad of problems associated with chronic and increasing unemployment, underemployment and low wages, it is time for the government to demonstrate its concern about the problem and its seriousness about finding solutions. We therefore recommend a high-level government Commission to Study and Propose Solutions to the Problem of Unemployment and Underemployment. This commission would hold hearings in various parts of the nation, consult with experts, take testimony from the unemployed and underemployed and report its findings and recommendations to the nation. It would contribute to public recognition of the problem of unemployment and hence to support for a more vigorous effort to expand employment opportunities. Possible models for such a commission include a Presidential commission or a bipartisan, tripartite commission established by joint resolution of the Congress. It is, in any case, important that groups suffering from unemployment and underemployment be represented on such a national body. We also recommend that subcommittees of the Commission be appointed to study and make recommendations for programs to help groups and regions with special needs, such as the rural poor, displaced or endangered family farmers, farmworkers, Appalachians and Native Americans.

Revising the Unemployment Measure

Unemployment is high during good times and bad. During the entire period since World War II, the United States avoided a major depression on the scale of the 1930s, but unemployment rates have only gone as low as 3 percent during periods of war—leaving millions without access to gainful employment, regardless of the business cycle. With each succeeding decade average unemployment rates have risen, from a low of 4.5 percent in the 1950s to 7.3 percent in the 1980s. While the United States collects little data on job vacancy rates (unlike other countries), what research has been conducted suggests that the number of job-seekers far exceeds the number of available jobs. The author of one such study, Katherine Abraham, now Commissioner of the U.S. Bureau of Labor Statistics (BLS), estimates that there were roughly 2.4 unemployed persons for every vacant job during the middle 1960s, when the official unemployment rate averaged 4.5 percent; an average of close to four unemployed persons per vacant job during the early 1970s, when unemployment averaged 5 percent; an average of five or more unemployed persons for every vacant job during the latter part of the 1970s, when unemployment averaged 6 to 7 percent; and an average of 8.4 persons for every vacant job in 1982, when unemployment was 9.5 percent.

High as it is, the official unemployment rate reported by the press masks much of the problem. For example, according to the BLS, in 1992 official joblessness averaged 7.4 percent, representing an annual average of 9.4 million persons. Another survey, also by the BLS, but not highlighted by the media, shows that 21.4 million persons were jobless *sometime during that year*. Unemployment is not evenly spread in the population, however. While three out of four of the unemployed are white, minorities are disproportionately unemployed. In 1992, African Americans had a depression-level unemployment rate of 14.1 percent, more than double the 6.5 percent rate for whites, and Hispanics had a rate of 11.4 percent. A disproportionate amount of minority joblessness is not revealed even by these figures.

The main reason why the official average rate seriously underestimates the magnitude of the jobless problem stems from the way people are classified in the labor force survey, which is the source of our figures. Persons working one or more hours weekly for pay or profit (or 15 hours of nonpaid employment for a family enterprise) are counted as employed, even if they are working part time but want full-time work; and nonemployed persons who want jobs but are not actively seeking work are counted as out of the labor force, rather than unemployed. Persons who have not "looked for work" in the past four weeks are not considered unemployed, regardless of their desire for work. "Looking for work" is based on a strict activity test—for example, persons placing or answering a want ad are considered "actively looking for work." However, looking at want ads but not applying for any job is not considered "looking for work," even if there are no jobs advertised for which the unemployed person would qualify.

A more realistic concept of unemployment is needed to estimate the extent of both official and hidden unemployment. In 1992, such an expanded concept would have included the 9.4 million people who were officially jobless, *plus* 6.4 million persons who wanted full-time jobs but were involuntarily forced to settle for part-time work (on the average for 20 hours weekly). It also would have included *all* 6.2 million persons who wanted jobs but were not actively looking for them. This group, comprised disproportionately of women, African Americans and Hispanics, consists of: a) 1.1 million officially designated discouraged workers—so tagged only when discouragement is the sole reason they were not seeking work; and b) 5.1 million more persons who wanted jobs but were not actively seeking them because of other reasons—for example, disabilities or home responsibilities. Even if discouragement is also a reason—but not the *sole* one—the latter are not considered discouraged workers. These statistically hidden unemployed persons wanted jobs and could have worked had there been enough additional jobs *and* sufficient support systems to provide rehabilitation and workplace redesign, an adequate supply of affordable child care, disabled-friendly transportation, and the like.

Using this expanded concept we find that an average of 22 million persons—more than double the 9.4 million officially unemployed—were either fully or partially jobless in 1992. A more limited approach that only includes involuntary part-timers and officially discouraged workers (excluding others who want jobs) shows that around 17 million were fully or partially jobless. Until 1994, a variant of the latter approach was available from the BLS. It was the most expansive of a range of unemployment rates based on differing definitions of unemployment that the BLS regularly provided.

That BLS variant, which got too little attention, was useful and should be reinstated. But our expanded concept provides further insights needed to understand and develop an inclusive full employment strategy, because it zeroes in on the need to create more jobs *and* to remove other barriers that prevent many people who want to work from doing so. Statistical measures that utilize variants of this expanded concept provide realistic measures of open and hidden unemployment. The National Urban League regularly calculates its "hidden unemployment index" using this approach, as does the Council on International and Public Affairs with its "joblessness rate."

For some groups, the obstacles to employment are so pervasive that the official labor force survey scarcely scratches the surface of their desire to work and their need for jobs. For example, according to a 1987 Harris poll commissioned by the International Center for the Disabled, almost 8.5 million working-age disabled persons wanted jobs, but due to near-insurmountable barriers, most did not engage in a job search. That number far exceeds the BLS estimate of 1 million job-wanting, but non-job-seeking disabled—none of them even considered discouraged workers.

It is well known that urban slums are replete with hidden unemployment; so are Native American reservations. Sar Levitan and Elizabeth Miller note that the Bureau of Indian Affairs (BIA) rejects the BLS definition as a poor indicator of unemployment on reservations. The BIA estimates jobless rates of from 40 to 60 percent on the 10 largest reservations (January 1991) compared to from 14 to 35 percent (April 1990) estimated by those using the BLS definition.

As noted, our expanded concept shows 22 million persons either fully or partially jobless in 1992. However, it would not have required 22 million additional full-time equivalent jobs to have filled this gap. This is because involuntary part-time workers only need more hours and some job-seekers may want part-time work. Also, in an economy such as we aim for—with decreased joblessness, higher wages and family income, and greater income security—some persons presently forced into the labor market by dire necessity (for example, some parents of infants, and students whose parents are now jobless or poorly paid) might opt out of the labor force or reduce their hours if conditions improved.

The exact number of jobs needed for all who would want to work in a real full employment economy is not precisely known. This is because the U.S. economy has not operated at full employment since World War II, and because we do not have the necessary support systems in place to enable everyone who wants to work to do so. Also, in a full employment society, conditions that now nurture crime would abate. Currently, prisoners are excluded from all labor force statistics and are not even considered out of the labor force. Prisoners now number more than a million and are disproportionately from groups with high unemployment rates and poor labor market prospects, particularly young minority men. Aiding ex-offenders to attain lawful employment would increase the number of employment opportunities needed.

Any organization or aspiring social movement that wishes to place its issue on the agenda for social action must convince the public that its problem is widespread. An expanded unemployment concept that estimates the full extent of joblessness can raise public consciousness of the problem of unemployment and underemployment, create the political will for full employment policies, and provide better information to plan for full employment.

Starting in 1994, the BLS made extensive changes in the way it surveys the labor force and measures unemployment. The full impact of these changes is not yet known, but early studies suggest that the official jobless rate will rise somewhat. We welcome changes that bring hidden unemployment into the open. However, certain changes will further mask some of the hidden unemployment. For example, the number of officially discouraged workers will be considerably smaller. The reason is because now to be so classified, it is still necessary to be out of the labor force *solely because of discouragement; but, in addition, one has to have engaged in a job search within* the past year and be available for work immediately. Similarly, changes are reducing the number of involuntary part-time workers who will be counted. In the labor force survey there is a general deemphasis on persons who want to work but have not sought work within the past year or who are not available for work immediately. Yet this is vital and needed information.

We therefore call on the Bureau of Labor Statistics to: a) develop and *give equal prominence to another measure of unemployment* that would include *all* those who want to work but are not looking for it, as well as those who are employed part-time but want full-time work; b) call a conference with other interested parties to increase the availability and emphasis in the labor force survey of persons who want to work but have not sought it in the past year, or who are not immediately available for work.

Finally, we note that none of these measures, not even our expanded concept, speaks to the issue of low wages. Work should also mean a decent income but it is often simply a stepping stone to further poverty. In the mid-1960s, when unemployment was less than 4 percent, Willard Wirtz, then-Secretary of Labor, recognized the futility of using official unemployment figures alone to analyze the situation of workers in urban slums. Under his guidance the Labor Department developed a subemployment index that took into account not only official un-employment, discouragement and involuntary part-time work, but also other factors, including poverty wages. Intensive surveys were conducted in ten slum areas where subemployment ranged from 24 to 47 percent, but the project was never carried out nationally and never repeated. Yet Wirtz was clearly identifying an important problem. The Kerner Commission, which investigated the urban riots of the 1960s, concluded that widespread subemployment was a major contributing factor. In recent years low wage work has become widespread throughout the society. A subemployment index would give greater recognition to the need for jobs at decent wages. Thus, we call on the BLS to develop a composite subemployment index that would include, in addition to the officially jobless, discouraged workers, involuntary part-time workers and those employed at poverty wages.

An Expanded Concept of Full Employment

In basing employment needs on more realistic measures, JOBS FOR ALL sets ambitious goals for full employment. Our expanded concept of unemployment is linked to an expanded concept of full employment, one similar to that of the original, but not the final, version of the Humphrey-Hawkins Full Employment and Balanced Growth Act. Many conceptions of full employment, even the pioneering work of Sir William Beveridge, have mainly had in mind the male population of working age, while others have assumed that large proportions of women, but not men, would be part-time workers. At the same time, our definition of work itself is a broad one that includes, values and compensates the care and nurture of the very young and the infirm by members of their own families.

Providing employment opportunities to the disabled and removing barriers to their participation in the work force have also been absent from most earlier conceptions of full employment. Both commitments to the disabled are included in JOBS FOR ALL.

Particularly in a nation with such a high crime rate, removing barriers to the employment of ex-offenders must also be part of full employment. Accordingly we proposed that ex-offenders be offered education, training and transitional or permanent jobs, if need be, to prevent them from returning to criminal occupations.

Full employment also includes equal access to jobs and occupational mobility for all workers. Such measures as affirmative action and pay equity are integral to real full employment. When we say, JOBS FOR ALL, that is precisely what we mean. A goal that includes jobs at decent wages for all who want to work is a moral as well as a political necessity if our society is to be an inclusive rather than a divisive one. This goal is also needed if we are to unleash the productive power of our people to improve our own and the world's quality of life.

Full Employment: The Key to Poverty and Crime Reduction

Unemployment rates are very high for young people, especially African Americans and Hispanics. In 1993, when the unemployment rate was 6.8 percent among 16 to 19-year olds in the labor force, nearly four in 10 African Americans and more than one in four Hispanics were jobless, compared to slightly more than one in six whites; and only about one-fourth of African Americans and one-third of Hispanics that age were employed, compared to nearly one-half of whites. For those who lack opportunities for steady, adequate employment or access to public assistance, the penal system may be serving as the social welfare system. With unemployment levels in a chronic state of crisis and virtually no public assistance, it is not surprising that on any one day in 1989 almost one-fourth of African American men between 20 and 29 were either in prison, jail, or on probation or parole. In his time Thomas Paine wrote, "Age goes to the poorhouse and youth to the gallows." In our time, there have been great strides against poverty among the elderly. Yet, in the nation for which the author of *The Rights of Man* had such high hopes, the modern equivalent of "youth to the gallows" persists. While not the entire answer to the crime and violence that plague our society, an ample supply of decent paying jobs would deter many youths from embarking on criminal careers.

Fortunately, there are recent, convincing data to sustain our claim that full employment would reduce poverty and increase the labor force participation of disadvantaged groups, particularly young men of color. A study by Paul Osterman found that after years of sustained economic growth and "full employment" in Boston, poverty rates fell by 36 percent for all families and by more than 50 percent for African American families (1980-1988). The drop in the poverty of unrelated individuals was even more precipitous. Another study, by Richard B. Freeman, found that in metropolitan statistical areas with unemployment rates under 4 percent in 1987, rates of unemployment had declined from 15.4 percent in 1980 to 5.7 percent four years later for all young men with 12 years of schooling or less, and from 40.5 percent to 7.2 percent for undereducated African American youth, a more than fivefold drop. At the same time, employment-population ratios rose, especially for African American youth (from 43 percent to 73 percent). Freeman estimates that for the country as a whole the reduction of youth unemployment to the level of those areas that had unemployment rates under 4 percent would require a national unemployment rate of 3 to 4 percent. These studies refute the myth that the so-called "underclass" is so beset with behavioral deficits that it is not able to respond to expanded employment opportunities. Further evidence that inner-city youth would take jobs if they were available is found periodically in newspaper stories which tell of thousands lining up for a few hundred job openings when such jobs are offered to this population.

Increased Public Investment

JOBS FOR ALL requires macroeconomic policies that would both stimulate job creation and spur economic growth through public investment. The United States cannot afford the human and economic waste of continued neglect of public investment. What Robert Heilbroner calls "the ferocious gutting of our public capital without precedent or purpose" has much to do with our economic decline and contributes substantially to a much lower rate of productivity growth than any of our major industrial competitors—all of which invest at rates that are twice or more those of the United States. Japan, for example, invested at 20 times the rate of the United States in recent years and achieved six times the U.S. productivity growth. According to the research of David Aschauer, which has been corroborated by other investigators, a dollar spent for public investment raises gross national product by two to five times the amount of a dollar spent for private investment. In short, we cannot afford not to invest in jobs and growth (see Section 6, "Environmental Sustainability," where we address what we mean by "growth").

Public civilian investment is more labor intensive than equivalent military spending and should offset cutbacks in defense. Seymour Melman estimates that a transfer of $165 billion from the military to education, infrastructure, environment, housing, health care, civilian research and development, etc. would lead to a net gain of 750,000 new U.S. jobs. Several million more jobs could be created with revenues raised by restoring 1980 tax levels on the highest income groups. These two job creation measures would not add a penny to the federal deficit in the short run.

From calculations of the Congressional Budget Office (CBO), we infer that reductions in unemployment and increases in economic growth would lead to substantial reductions in the federal deficit. The reason is that revenues would expand and expenditures decrease. Extrapolating from CBO estimates, if unemployment had gone up an additional percentage point in fiscal year 1993, the first-year increase in the deficit would have been around $45 billion (see Section 10, "Sound Government Finance"). If that one percentage point increase in unemployment were to be sustained, the deficit would nonetheless increase each year because of the accumulating debt service.

Direct Government Job Creation

While we envision that public investment in the private sector would greatly expand jobs in that sector, direct creation of jobs by the federal government will also be necessary. Indeed, we recommend that public employment programs provide employment for all those who seek gainful work but are unable to find it. In effect, this would establish an entitlement to work.

Since the 1930s, the federal government has undertaken job creation, but not on a continuous basis. In order to reduce the mass unemployment of the Great Depression, the New Deal launched a number of public works and public employment programs to provide employment to a portion of the jobless. At their heights in 1934 and 1938, these New Deal work programs employed 4.6 million persons, or nearly one out of every three of the unemployed. These public employment programs built some of the nation's largest and best known public works, including hundreds of thousands of miles of new and improved roads, the construction or renovation of hundreds of thousands of bridges and viaducts, and thousands of new public buildings, stadiums, parks, playgrounds, and athletic fields. Many unemployed musicians, artists, actors, dancers, playwrights and others developed programs enjoyed by millions. The Writers Project endowed the country with lasting works and helped launch the careers of some of our most important authors. The theater, the music world and dance were permanently enriched by these products, and much important historical knowledge (such as the slave narratives) was preserved through the oral history that was collected.

Despite the belief of leading New Dealers that public employment should be part of a permanent program of economic security and their stated preference for work relief rather than direct relief, the Social Security Act made provision for the latter but not the former. Work relief programs were discontinued in the 1940s, when the government employed millions directly in the armed forces and stimulated the employment of millions more through war contracts. Among other things, World War II was a massive employment program that created full employment for the first and only time during this century. However, as we show, in Section 5, "Military Conversion," full employment can and should be achieved without massive military expenditures.

The history of public job creation since the Great Depression reveals that the United States government, in spite of a rhetoric which emphasizes the work ethic, has been far more willing to establish entitlements to welfare or income transfer programs than to work. The major federal income support programs, Social Security and public assistance, have operated continuously and expanded significantly since 1935. Despite rising unemployment in the 1950s, there were no public job creation efforts until some limited experiments were initiated in the 1960s. The New Frontier included a public employment program employing, at peak, 46,000 persons, as well as some smaller programs targeted to impoverished areas, disadvantaged youth and the elderly. Higher unemployment in the 1970s brought a short-lived Emergency Employment Act, and later in the decade, the largest public employment program since the Depression, the Comprehensive Employment and Training Act (CETA), which employed over 752,000 persons in 1978. Sar Levitan and Frank Gallo note that opponents of CETA falsely identified the effort in the public mind with incompetence and corruption. Major studies, however, found that the overwhelming majority of these activities were beneficial and there was little fraud or abuse. Nevertheless, CETA was abruptly terminated in 1981. Soon after, however, in response to the highest rate of unemployment since the 1930s, some modest programs, emphasizing training instead of employment, were initiated.

The record of federal job creation programs is a very positive one that conflicts sharply with the efforts by opponents to discredit them. Drawing on an impressive knowledge of the literature, including an authoritative study by Clifford Johnson for the House Committee on Education and Labor, Levitan and Gallo emphasize the value of jobs programs in reducing unemployment, replacing welfare with work, supplying needed services, and enhancing participants' subsequent earnings. Echoing the title of Harry Hopkins' book on the massive work programs that he administered as part of the New Deal, Levitan's and Gallo's 1992 study, entitled, *Spending to Save*, calls for a jobs program in bad and good times. In another important study, *Securing the Right to Employment*, Philip Harvey has made a cogent argument for a government guaranteed jobs program for all employable persons of working age in the United States. Harvey anticipates that the program he proposes would not increase the long-term tax burden.

We recommend a permanent, standby job creation program by the federal government. Initially, job creation should be equivalent to half the number of the officially unemployed. Subsequently, the government should move toward complete coverage of the jobless. Much direct job creation, it should be emphasized, would be a public investment that would build both the human and physical resources on which future productivity depends.

Expanding Federal Support for the Arts

A significant measure of the level of culture in a developed society is the status accorded its visual and performing arts. Culture is one of the United States' hottest export items. Yet excessive commercialization has often impeded the quality of U.S. cultural products, has placed quality visual and performing arts beyond the financial reach of the majority of Americans, has made chronic unemployment the way of life for many aspiring artists, writers and performers, and has discouraged many others from even developing their creative talents in the first place.

In many other countries, state support for the arts is far greater than it is in the United States. To meet the need for access to artistic quality, to encourage the full development of the creative potential of more Americans, and to provide jobs in the arts, we call for increased federal funding for the arts. Such funding, to be secured through federal budget commitment, as well as through ticket and art sales, could help to support a national theater, modeled somewhat after the national theater in Great Britain. Such a theater would have local units scattered in towns and cities throughout the United States to train new actors, musicians, and dancers, to give performance outlets to new writers, and to provide entry to the arts for millions of Americans at prices they could afford. Support for the visual arts should be for small galleries and cooperative art studios. Enhanced commitment to the arts would have a job multiplier effect. With each new artist who is supported there would be increased demand for supplies and technical equipment.

Reducing Work Time

While increasing numbers of Americans face unemployment and underemployment, others are working longer hours at more jobs. As Juliet Schor has written, the proportion of workers who cannot work as many hours as they would like has more than doubled in the last 20 years and, in the same period, total annual hours of labor force participation have increased by the equivalent of an extra month of work. The existence of such unevenness in workforce participation could be eased by equitable forms of work-sharing that would contribute to job creation as well as allow more time for family, community life and leisure. Certain types of workers, for example, some disabled and older workers, parents of young children or those who must take care of sick or elderly relatives, could be given the option of reduced work time at commensurately reduced pay. Beyond that, we propose a staged reduction of the standard work week with hours reduced to a level that would be commensurate with full employment.

Such proposals are not new. During the Great Depression, a broad coalition of groups, including labor leaders and the Secretary of Labor, seriously considered a 30-hour work week with no reduction in pay, in order to spread the work around. We also propose statutory vacation time for all workers, including contingent workers, and sabbaticals for all permanent workers. Since 1980, vacation time has shrunk in the United States, even though it has continued to increase for European workers. Some state governments have reduced the costs of work sharing by making unemployment insurance benefits available to workers who reduce their work time. These workers receive pay for the time they work and unemployment benefits for their days of joblessness, thus preventing the layoff of their colleagues. We recommend that a national program extend such measures.

Taking into account data from European research, which found that reduced work time results in productivity gains, we recognize that the number of jobs created through such policies would be less than the number of hours reduced. Moving from the standard work week of 40 hours to 36 would result in a job increase of three to four percent (rather than 10 percent). The increased productivity is important; so are the gains in jobs for the unemployed and time for those who are employed but overworked. The wage increases proposed as part of Principle 2 should make work reduction more acceptable to lower-income groups. Overall reductions in work time are a more equitable form of work sharing than the present inequitable distribution of jobs—overemployment for some and unemployment and involuntary part-time employment for others.

The poor distribution of work is abetted by some government policies. As Juliet Schor points out, employers' contributions to Social Security, unemployment insurance and other programs are capped. After a certain level of earnings is reached, no further taxes are levied. This creates a bias toward requiring more hours from existing workers rather than adding new workers, which would add to the tax bill. The taxable wage base for Social Security has risen considerably over the years, but not so for unemployment insurance. We propose, therefore, that all employer payroll taxes be levied on all overtime earnings, even if a worker's earnings already exceed the maximum taxable limit. We also propose raising the legally mandated rate for overtime under the Fair Labor Standards Act and extending its coverage in order to further discourage firms from using overtime. Another option would be to put some limits on overtime except where labor shortages exist. However, these actions must be taken in conjunction with new legislative protection of wage and benefit standards, including health benefits, for all part-time and other contingent workers. This is needed in the interest of simple justice—and to prevent employers from substituting more part-time and other contingent workers at lower wages and without fringe benefits. A national universal health coverage plan is a necessary part of such a policy.

Full Employment and Inflation

In proposing a JOBS FOR ALL program, we are fully aware that the nation has long eschewed a policy with much to recommend it in both human and economic terms. Except during wartime, the United States has consistently sacrificed full employment—and with it the dignity and well-being of millions of its citizens—in order to control inflation. The U.S. pledges allegiance to the work ethic while deliberately creating and sustaining slack in labor markets through restrictive monetary policies. However, the correlation between rising employment and inflation is now disputed. Indeed, the term "stagflation" was coined in the 1970s to highlight the convergence of both inflation and a stagnating, high-unemployment economy. Though the choice between employment or inflation is often presented as one of economic necessity, the decision is largely a political one, reflecting the lack of power of those who experience unemployment or the lower wages and deteriorating working conditions that are its indirect effects. As the Kreisky Commission (named for its chair, former Austrian premier Bruno Kreisky) reported to the European Community (EC), "unemployment is a political problem, not an economic one."

Since the Congressional Budget Office (CBO) expects inflation rates to remain flat at about 2.75 percent through 1994, our thoughts at ᐧthis time should be trained on other, more pressing, economic problems. However, in view of the severe political consequences of the fear of inflation, it is important to emphasize that countries that are committed to full employment have means for controlling inflation other than the restrictive, disemploying monetary policies preferred by the United States.

At this time, when inflation is not a major economic problem, it is important to undertake long-term efforts that would enable the nation to cope more effectively with it. An important step would be to develop the kind of tripartite cooperation among business, labor, and government that has helped to control inflation in some other capitalist economies. Of course, such a measure would depend upon and, in turn, facilitate the organized power of workers.

The Swedish experiment is also useful here. Over many decades Swedish policymakers aimed to attain full employment and to control inflation. Part of their strategy was to avoid overreliance on general expansionary policies that might cause inflationary bottlenecks without getting at the most stubborn unemployment. Thus they developed an extensive *active* labor market policy to concentrate on enabling the jobless to work, rather than a *passive* policy of focusing on income support for the jobless. The policy mix has varied over time but has included such approaches as: extensive labor market training; special programs for disadvantaged groups and regions; job creation; an innovative employment service with mandatory job listings and a national computerized network; and mobility grants to enable workers to take jobs in areas with greater employment opportunity.

Active labor market policy is not the whole answer to achieving either full employment or low inflation but can play an important role. For many decades Sweden had considerably lower unemployment than most countries, including the United States, averaging 1.7 percent in the 1960s, 2 percent in the 1970s and 2.5 percent in the 1980s (adjusted to U.S. measurement methods). And during part of this period—for example in the 1970s—its inflation was less than the average for the OECD European nations, though more than in the United States. However, in the 1990s, under a newly elected conservative government, its unemployment was pushed up in order to "harmonize" the economy downward prior to joining the European Union.

In the United States, job training programs are notoriously ill-matched to jobs. We propose research to determine how many jobs are actually vacant, where jobs are located and what kinds of skills they require. Any allegations by industry of shortages in particular sectors of the labor market must be carefully examined for their accuracy. Rather than expanding immigration quotas to fill labor market shortages, government must ensure that every effort be made to train unemployed or underemployed native workers to fill such slots, as well as ensure that the rights of immigrant workers be vigorously enforced.

Recognizing the political consequences of the fear of inflation, we call attention to other inflation-controlling measures that might be considered by policymakers. One such approach recommends direct controls on prices, profits, executive salaries, professional fees and wages. Such controls are much decried as an added bureaucratic burden; but, in our view—and from the perspective of the World War II experience with full employment and controls—they are a small price to pay for a *nation that works*. Organized labor is not fundamentally opposed to wage and price controls but is concerned lest controls be imposed on workers' wages but not on upper-income salaries. Recognizing the decline in wages that has taken place in the last two decades and the upward distribution of income to the privileged, we believe it important that controls, if deemed necessary, be equitably applied so as not to harm those with modest incomes who have lost ground over the last two decades. Some inflation-curbing measures that have been suggested include an anti-inflation tax incentive, such as a tax on corporations signing an inflationary wage settlement or, failing that, a direct inflation-geared tax on incomes or consumption. Abba Lerner has suggested a market in rights to raise prices. Those businesses wishing to raise prices would be required to purchase the right to do so from those proposing to lower prices. Recently, William Vickrey proposed a variant of this scheme, namely, tradeable or "marketable growth markup warrants," with penalties or taxes for those firms retaining fewer warrants than the excess of sales revenues over amounts paid for non-prime inputs in the preceding period.

Anti-Discrimination Policies and Full Employment

Full employment strengthens the position of labor generally, but it does not in itself overcome the group inequalities stemming from discrimination based on race, national origin, ethnicity, gender, age, disability and sexual orientation. Indeed, in the absence of measures to reduce inequality, disadvantaged groups would remain in the same relative position with respect to education, training and occupational status. Full employment, therefore, is a necessary but not a sufficient condition for overcoming inequality in the labor market.

Accordingly, JOBS FOR ALL must incorporate a renewed commitment to the enforcement of anti-discrimination laws, notably the Equal Pay Act of 1963, Title VII of the Civil Rights Act of 1964, as amended and expanded by the Civil Rights Act of 1991, the Age Discrimination in Employment Act of 1967 as amended, the Pregnancy Discrimination Act of 1978, and implementation of affirmative action policies set forth in various Executive Orders. Title I of the Americans with Disabilities Act of 1990 must be vigorously enforced and its promise of equal opportunities must be translated into actual jobs for all the disabled by other governmental measures that go beyond present law, such as comprehensive support services and job development. Pay equity, (or comparable worth) laws, which have been enacted in some states and which pertain only to public employment, should be extended to federal and private sectors. With respect to sexual harassment in the workplace, the Equal Employment Opportunity Commission (EEOC) needs to change its definition of the offense so as to place the burden of proof and responsibility on the accused offenders rather than on the plaintiffs or victims. State laws against sexual harassment in the workplace and procedures for implementing these laws also need to be strengthened. New legislation to ban employment discrimination on the basis of sexual orientation should also be passed.

A special unit in the Department of Labor should be created to disseminate information about opportunities for employment, promotion, and training and to coordinate the efforts of government, private sector and community-based organizations to achieve an appropriate match between individuals and jobs. Such an agency would contribute to the goal of employment equity by preparing educational material explaining that everyone benefits when homelessness, poverty and unemployment are conquered.

Full Employment and the Globalization of Capital

The globalization of capital that has resulted in the loss of millions of U.S. jobs clearly makes the task of achieving full employment more difficult. Elsewhere (see Section 4, "Community Investment, Preservation and Support") we call for a policy of "stay or pay" that would restrain businesses that have profited from the nation's human and material resources from simply escaping the labor and environmental laws for which generations of Americans have struggled. Such a policy would either keep more jobs here or provide resources that could be used for job creation and training of displaced workers.

The globalization of capital has made a large public jobs program all the more necessary. Such a program serves the important purpose of rebuilding our neglected public infrastructure and increases the ability of presently disadvantaged workers to consume the products and services of the private sector. As a rule of thumb it is thought that for each job created in the public sector, another will be instituted in the market sector.

As in the national economy, increasing the purchasing power of those at the bottom is required in the global economy. The Trade Union Advisory Committee to the Organization for Economic Cooperation and Development (OECD) has suggested the need for a global "New Deal." Ultimately, the response to the globalization of capital should be a policy of full employment in all nations and the extension to developing countries of industrial-country labor standards, collective bargaining rights and environmental protection (see Section 4, "Community Investment, Preservation and Support" and Section 7, "Fair Trade and Economically Viable Local Production for Local Consumption"). Such a global "New Deal," or global Keynesianism, would require international cooperation and coordination of monetary, fiscal and trade policies aimed at increasing employment on a scale far greater than any nation has yet shown itself willing to assume. Yet the beginnings of that cooperation are there in several of the international treaties and covenants cited in this book. Adherence to International Labour Organisation (ILO) standards and these several international agreements by *all* nations, including the United States and developing countries, would go a long way toward such cooperation.

A first step would be for the United States to accept and adhere to conventions of the ILO on child labor, the rights of unions and workplace health and safety. As a second indication of our nation's commitment to economic democracy, the Senate should approve without extensive reservations the International Covenant on Economic, Social and Cultural Rights, which was signed by President Carter, ratified by the other six leading industrialized countries (Britain, Canada, France, Germany, Italy, and Japan), and supported by Secretary of State Warren Christopher at the 1993 Vienna Human Rights Summit. Included in this Covenant's definition of universal rights are the "right to work" and "the right of everyone to the enjoyment of just and favorable conditions of work," which includes the following provisions: "fair wages" and "equal remuneration for work of equal value"; a "decent standard of living"; "safe and healthy working conditions"; "equal opportunity to promotion"; "rest, leisure and reasonable limitation of working hours"; "holidays with pay"; "the right to form and join trade unions and to strike" (Article 6). Also included are the right to "paid leave or leave with adequate social security benefits" for working mothers (Article 10); the "highest attainable standard of physical and mental health" (Article 12); and the right to education—including higher education (Article 13).

We recognize that many of these rights have been violated even by countries which have signed the Covenant. Nevertheless, the Covenant provides a useful set of criteria by which to measure any government's progress toward universally recognized standards. The Covenant requires ratifying governments to file reports with the international body of experts on enforcement of each of these rights, on reasons for their failure to enforce, and on concrete plans to increase enforcement. Citizens can then use the Covenant in litigation and as a tool for consciousness-raising and for mobilizing others both domestically and internationally to monitor, evaluate and prod their governments to make progress toward these goals.

To move us from lip service to action on a global New Deal, we suggest the convening, perhaps by the United Nations, of an international summit on employment, to discuss the need for and the mechanisms to accomplish greater cooperation on securing sustainable development with global full employment (see the Conclusion of JOBS FOR ALL for greater discussion of this proposal).

2.

ADEQUATE INCOME FOR ALL

JOBS FOR ALL establishes a goal of adequate income for everyone in the United States, to be derived primarily from earnings. The policy issues to be determined in achieving adequate income for all include: 1) the standard for adequate earnings or wages; and 2) the conditions under which income transfers should be available for persons of working age.

The Standard for Adequate Earnings

We suggest that initially the standard for the minimum wage be equivalent to that which the U.S. Census Bureau defines as "low annual earnings," namely the poverty standard for a family of four ($14,335 in 1992). This was equivalent to about $6.90 an hour at a time when the federal minimum wage was $4.25.

At an earlier time, when the nation had fewer economic resources (lower per capita GNP), we came closer to achieving the goal of an anti-poverty minimum wage. In 1968 the minimum wage was 94 percent of the four-person and 120 percent of the three-person poverty level.

A special Census Bureau study showed that in 1990, over 14 million people, or 18 percent of all workers who worked year-round, full-time (35 hours a week) had earnings below the poverty standard for a family of four. For Hispanics and African Americans the figures were 31 percent and 25 percent respectively, and for women, nearly one-fourth of full-time workers had low annual earnings. The Census Bureau also developed a concept of year-round, full-time *attachment* to the labor force, which includes, in addition to full-time, year-round workers, persons who spent at least 50 weeks during the year looking for work and those who worked fewer than 35 hours a week for nonvoluntary reasons. Using this more expanded concept, over one-fourth of all workers and one-third of women workers with year-round, full-time attachment to the labor force had low annual earnings in 1990.

While raising the minimum wage to the equivalent of the current poverty standard for a family of four would increase the earnings of millions of workers, it is important to point out that the poverty standard itself is an inadequate one. When devised in the middle 1960s, the standard was based on an Economy Food Plan for "temporary or emergency use when funds are low." Since some studies done in the 1950s found that lower-income families spent one third of their income on food, the poverty index was determined by multiplying the Economy Food Plan by three for families of three or more. The current formula simply adjusts the poverty threshold originally determined in this fashion for inflation. It is conventional to assume that families use 30 percent of their income for rent. Thirty percent of the poverty standard for a four-person family in 1992 was $4,300, or $358 a month, an amount well below fair-market rents for that size family in major urban areas. The relative cost of other household items, such as child care and transportation, have also risen in proportion to food.

Despite being based on an inadequate food budget and dubious assumptions about the relationship between food costs and total family consumption, the four-person poverty standard was originally equal to about one-half the median family income, often considered to be a better measure of poverty than an absolute standard. In 1992, however, the four-person budget was only 32 percent of the median family income for a four-person family.

The most recent and comprehensive analysis of the poverty standard was undertaken by Patricia Ruggles for the Joint Economic Committee of Congress. Ruggles concluded that the most pressing priority in poverty measurement is the need to update the consumption standards on which the poverty threshold is based. She agrees with some observers who argue that the Census Bureau should include at least part of the value of noncash transfer payments, such as food stamps, in determining whether incomes fall below the poverty level. However, she points out that the current U.S. poverty level would have to be at least 50 percent higher than at present to reflect actual changes in consumption standards. We also believe that in a nation as large and diverse as the United States, the poverty standard should reflect regional differences in the cost of living.

While JOBS FOR ALL proposes use of the current poverty standard as a basis for the minimum wage, we recognize the inadequacy of this standard. We recommend that the poverty standard itself be revised upward and that the minimum wage be adjusted accordingly. Another alternative would be to adopt the relative poverty standard of 50 percent of the median income, a figure that tends to be compatible with the amount that Americans believe to be an adequate minimum standard. Using either of these as the basis of the minimum wage would make it truly an antipoverty wage.

Support for Family Life

Even in a full-employment economy with adequate wages, certain forms of income support for persons of working age and their families will be necessary. If family members choose to care for the very young and the infirm themselves, they should be able to do so without undue financial hardship. We believe that it is the responsibility of government to provide support to family members who interrupt employment to perform work in the home. Government should also subsidize non-parental child care for children in the preschool years. Another function of social policy that remains important in a full-employment economy is to offset the increased costs of bearing and rearing children through some form of children's allowances. Finally, the meager support that children get from noncustodial parents must be addressed. Government needs to guarantee child support from noncustodial parents, or in cases of their default or inadequate incomes, to provide it through public funds.

The recently enacted unpaid family leave of 12 weeks is a step in the right direction. Yet it falls far short of what is needed and lags way behind what many other comparably developed countries already have. The next step toward recognizing the value of family care is to pay for family leave through income transfers. Some Western European nations have gone far in the direction of paid family leave. Germany now supplements paid parental leave with a paid child-rearing leave of 36 months, although at amounts insufficient for a single parent to support his or her family. In Sweden, either parent may have a government sponsored paid leave at 90 percent of earnings (up to a limit) for 12 months plus a flat rate for three more months. Ultimately, the goal in Sweden is for 18 months. As an initial goal, we propose that a paid leave for 12 months at an adequate replacement rate be phased in over a reasonable period of time. Ultimately, paid parental leave should be available for the first two years of a child's life. Paid leaves for the care of the disabled and infirm should also be available.

We propose that family care-givers have opportunities for job training or education to minimize losses in occupational development and mobility as a result of their absence from the labor market. These could be part of the "Lifelong Learning" proposals that are described at the end of this document (see Section 11). Such opportunities should be available in the evening when other family members can assume care of children or the disabled. Another option, if other family members are not available, is to offer some forms of on-site babysitting or respite care at educational and training sites.

The availability of nonparental child care reduces the interruption of employment and earnings. Since it is mothers who have usually assumed the major responsibility for child care and often at the cost of earnings and career mobility, the provision of quality child care is not only important to children. It is essential if women are to participate on an equal footing with men in a full employment economy. Indeed, child care is a step toward reducing gender equality in the workplace. We propose that universal, quality, subsidized child care be available in the preschool years, beginning at the age of two. One way to reduce the costs of paid parental leaves and child care subsidies is to treat benefits under these programs as earned income for tax purposes; we recommend such recoupment of benefits.

The JOBS FOR ALL program is intended to reduce the substantial amounts of single parenthood born of poverty—the results of chronic unemployment and low wages, particularly among young, minority men and women. Yet much single parenthood will undoubtedly remain. A major cause of poverty and low income among single-parent families is inadequate child support on the part of noncustodial parents. Although jobs at decent wages will make it possible for more noncustodial parents to meet their obligations, we believe that public subsidies will still be necessary if all children are to have adequate support. We recommend a policy similar to that which has been adopted in some other countries in which government establishes a minimum level of child support, determines how much the noncustodial parent can afford to pay and makes up the difference between the minimum and what the parent pays. In cases of willful default, government authorities attempt to collect the money through wage withholding and other sanctions. Sweden's experience with guaranteed child support underscores the need for public child-support subsidies, even in a full employment economy where a high proportion of parents meet their support obligations. Although about 85 percent of parental support obligations were paid in recent years, these represented only 35 percent of the costs of the program. An experiment modeled on Sweden's guaranteed child-support program is underway in Wisconsin and is being observed by Congress with a view toward nationwide adoption. In order to hold down the cost of this program, wc propose making such allowances part of taxable income.

Family allowances are a feature of the income-support systems of most industrialized countries. They are a recognition that parenthood and child rearing are services not only to one's family, but to the entire community, and that assuming parental responsibilities results in both extra expense and reduced earnings. Family allowances vary widely with respect to eligibility and benefit levels. Some countries provide substantial monthly payments to all children regardless of family income. Other countries restrict allowances to larger families and to those with low incomes. In order to preserve the principles of universality and fiscal prudence, we propose a modest monthly allowance, available to all children in a family, but subject to taxation.

It will take time to reach full employment and to reduce the need for means-tested public assistance. In this connection it is important to call attention to the experience of Sweden, whose government for many decades achieved near full employment at adequate wages and offered a range of generous family benefits, including paid parental leaves, subsidized child care and family allowances. Nonetheless, in 1985, about 40 percent of Swedish single mothers and their children received means-tested social assistance for an average of four and one-half months.

The Clinton administration favors the Earned Income Tax Credit (EITC) as a means of increasing the incomes of low-wage workers, primarily those with dependent children. In 1993, the EITC was significantly expanded. Although it is means tested, the EITC does not have the stigmatizing attributes of traditional public assistance. It is administered not by a local, often oppressive, welfare bureaucracy, but by the Internal Revenue Service, an agency that tests the incomes of all citizens, not simply those who are poor. We recognize that there are political advantages to paying benefits through the tax system at a time when increases in expenditures for the traditional welfare program are thought to be unpopular. Another argument that is sometimes made in favor of the EITC, which also applies to children's allowances, is that it permits the minimum wage to be pegged to an employee and one dependent, rather than to larger families.

It is important to point out, however, that the EITC offers no income support to the millions of persons who are unemployed. Nor does it cover those who leave the labor force as a result of illness, family care responsibilities or to escape oppressive working conditions. In addition to pointing out that the EITC is no help to those who are unemployed or out of the work force, Heidi Hartmann and Roberta Spalter-Roth of the Institute for Women's Policy Research hold that some recipients of Aid to Families of Dependent Children (AFDC), who combine earnings and AFDC benefits, would be worse off with a combination of earnings and EITC benefits.

The EITC is no help to the very groups for whom income support has become more restrictive and less generous in the last decades. For example, according to the Center on Social Welfare Policy and Law, the average AFDC benefit in 1992 was less than 66 percent of the 1975 average benefit level, and the combined benefits from AFDC and food stamps were below 79 percent of the poverty level in all but four states, none of which provided benefits equivalent to the poverty line. (Despite the level to which welfare benefits have shrunk, increases in these meager benefits are utterly absent from the agenda of welfare *reform*.)

NIFE supports efforts to increase the incomes of low-wage employees but is mindful that the EITC could be a subsidy to low-wage employers. To the extent that it increases labor force participation in the low-wage sector, the EITC could also contribute to a further decline in wages. The EITC could reduce incentives to increase the minimum wage (as could the children's allowance, for that matter). In this context, we point out that the Clinton Administration, while proposing a substantial increase in the EITC, has not met its campaign promises to push for higher wages or increases in the federal minimum wage. Although the EITC increases the incomes of the working poor, our preference is for a policy of jobs for all at wages that provide adequate support to workers and their families.

Other Income Support Programs for Workers

In a full-employment economy, the need for unemployment insurance will be quite minimal. Recognizing that it will take some time to achieve full employment, and that even at full employment there will be some frictional unemployment, we recommend strengthening the unemployment insurance (UI) system as an income safety net and as a counter-cyclical tool to help the economy by maintaining consumer purchasing power. In most non-recessionary years, little more than one-third of the jobless receive any unemployment benefits and these average only about one-third of prior earnings. Many exhaust their benefits before finding work, while others do not qualify for benefits. Minorities and women, both disproportionately represented in the contingent workforce, are among those hurt by such provisions and are less likely to collect benefits when jobless. All wage and salary workers should be covered by UI and harsh and excessive eligibility and disqualification provisions should be eliminated. Also, reentrants to the labor force should be covered. This exclusion hits women especially hard. Benefit levels need to be increased substantially and should be extended to 65 weeks. As in many other countries, the coverage should be even longer for some older workers. After a lifetime of work, many of them have little chance of reemployment and are too young to collect Social Security retirement benefits.

While a universal health insurance program would obviate the loss of coverage now encountered by many unemployed workers, health benefits should be available to the unemployed through unemployment insurance. Our preference, of course, is for an emphasis on the creation of jobs and on health benefits for all, regardless of employment status or income.

Although insurance against job loss will be greatly diminished in a full-employment economy, workers will still need to be insured against various forms of disability. The national Disability Insurance (DI) program that insures workers against permanent disability and the state Workers Compensation programs that insure against work-connected injury and illness need to be continued and strengthened. Insurance against temporary, non-work-connected disability is only available in a handful of states. We recommend the establishment of a national insurance program to cover temporary, non-work-related disability, including maternity.

3.

RIGHTS OF WORKERS

The labor policies of both the government and employers have contributed to the dramatic erosion of union membership—down to 15.8 percent of the labor force in 1992 (11.5 percent of workers in the private sector), compared to 32.5 percent at its height in 1953. The structures of protection and representation that were the objectives of the National Labor Relations Act of 1935 (The Wagner Act) have been badly weakened, starting with the 1947 Taft-Hartley Act which should be repealed. The erosion of labor's power is reflected in declining wages and benefits; longer working hours; the return of nineteenth century conditions such as child labor and sweatshops; alarming increases in industrial accidents and the loss of a sense of solidarity. Moreover, the increasing globalization of investment and production, new technologies that accelerate the displacement of workers across every sector of the economy simultaneously, and changes in the composition of the workforce require not only that we remedy damages already inflicted, but redesign laws, regulations and enforcement mechanisms to take these new developments into account.

Strengthening Workers' Bargaining and Wage Rights

The conceptual and factual basis of the Wagner Act was recognition of the inherent inequality of capital and labor and the need for positive government action to address this inequality. Two assumptions governed: 1) workers will choose union representation in most cases, provided that their choices are free and uncoerced; and 2) employers should have *no* voice or role in the choices workers make. These principles are also affirmed by the International Covenant on Civil and Political Rights, ratified by the United States in 1992.

The law must be reframed to reflect these assumptions, and it must be administered by a National Labor Relations Board that is committed to fair enforcement. Among the issues which need attention are unduly long preelection deliberations to define the unit of representation and the establishment of election rules and timetables. The latter include: expediting decisions through the use of card-checks to validate outcomes in order to avoid the time and cost of an election; prompt resolution of union and employer objections and prompt certification when majorities choose union representation; and enforcement of the obligation to negotiate in good faith and to incorporate the results in written, binding agreements within a short time after a successful election.

There is also an urgent need for legislation to reverse the Supreme Court decision permitting employers to hire permanent replacements for striking workers. Without such legislation, unions can offer virtually no protection to their members during strikes.

One of the original purposes of the Fair Labor Standards Act (the wage and hour law) was to limit overtime work, thereby providing more employment to people, especially the unemployed. Employers frequently prefer to use employed workers more intensively rather than to hire more workers. The law needs to be changed in order to strengthen the original incentives for limiting overtime and to make them effective. As we have already shown, one way would be to increase the legally mandated rate of overtime pay (see Section 1, "Jobs for All").

Related legislation is also needed to protect the large numbers of part-time and temporary workers, many of whom receive lower hourly pay rates than full-time, permanent workers and few, if any, benefits. The law should guarantee hourly wage parity among all workers doing the same job. These contingent workers should also be covered by all labor legislation and be entitled to pro-rated fringe benefits. Any health care system that is enacted should be universal and grant the same coverage to all, regardless of work status.

In recent years, some employers have unilaterally revoked agreements to provide fringe benefits to workers in their retirement. These are earned rights which should be legally guaranteed. Some form of vested entitlement to these benefits should be legally insured and protected.

Strengthening Workers' Health and Safety Protection

Job-based hazards include violation of safety and ecological standards, stress arising from job pressures and job insecurity. Government agencies for protecting health and safety at work have been weakened in recent years by funding and enforcement cutbacks. Today they lag far behind in the task of protecting workers and the public from current workplace dangers. At a minimum, these agencies must be upgraded with better funding, better and larger staffs and greater power to assess and act swiftly on health and safety hazards.

New legislation is needed to require the makers and distributors of substances and technical devices to provide full information for assessing any potential hazards to health and safety, to require that all workers be informed about them, and to empower workers to act in cases where there is reason to believe their health or safety is at risk. Official agencies for testing, assessment and inspection serve as the administrative bodies with the knowledge and power to judge whether such actions once taken should be continued or not. Safe destruction of a device, when it malfunctions or becomes obsolete, should be a condition for receipt of a patent.

Strengthening Workers' Voices in Workplace Decisions

In addition to strengthening protection and bargaining rights, measures should be taken to strengthen workers' voices in workplace decision-making. Experience in Scandinavia and West Germany and some limited experience in the United States demonstrates that full participation in decision-making, at the level of the workplace and the enterprise itself, both enhances employment security and improves efficiency and productivity. Experience also shows that without legally enforceable rights, participation systems unilaterally designed or introduced by employers can be exploitative and can reduce job security. Authentic participation is therefore best encouraged by appropriate legislative provisions, adapted from such sources as the German co-determination law and the Swedish democratization law. Workers should be able to participate in decisions pertaining to alternative production methods and technologies, geographic shifting, consolidation and reorganization of patterns of operations. When these affect workers' job security, job prospects, earnings, retirement or other benefit packages, they should be disclosed and discussed with the workers and their elected representatives prior to final decisions and their implementation. Beyond that, the law might well incorporate incentives designed to stabilize employment levels, provide entry and upward mobility opportunities for members of disadvantaged groups, and enable workers to be educated and trained to adapt to changes in methods or organization of work.

The Changing Composition of the Labor Force

Large numbers of new entrants into the labor market are people of color and immigrants, many from disadvantaged backgrounds. Labor laws and regulations must recognize the changing composition of the workforce so as not to disadvantage these new entrants.

As provided in the United Nations International Covenant on Civil and Political Rights, the right of workers to use their own language on the job should be established unless employers can show that using standard English is job-related and required by business necessity. Stated job requirements should eliminate criteria which are not demonstrably job-related and necessary for the safe and efficient operation of the business. This is especially the case when majority culture assumptions are embodied, often unconsciously, in such requisites as height, language comprehension and general knowledge. By the same token, for immigrants who wish to learn English, there should be an adequate supply of free, conveniently located and educationally viable English instruction classes.

Since it is clear that the immigration law does not prevent the hiring of undocumented workers, such workers should be entitled to full protection of all labor statutes and to all provisions of negotiated contracts between unions and employers.

4.

COMMUNITY INVESTMENT,

PRESERVATION AND SUPPORT

Many products are the work of communities. Productive enterprises do not exist in a vacuum. Corporations are chartered by communities and are situated within communities which depend on them and on which they, in turn, depend. These mutual dependencies hold even when corporations lie within urban or metropolitan areas where the particular community from which their workers come cannot be easily identified. The community provides a productive workforce, physical infrastructure, police and fire protection, basic education and training for the work force, and, in many cases, tax subsidies. The community permits employers and corporate owners to avoid individual responsibility for their decisions and even for violations of many laws by forming imaginary entities treated as "persons" in the law. In return, the corporation provides employment and income to the community.

Corporate Citizenship

These mutual dependencies carry responsibilities as well as benefits. The community has developed certain modes of living which depend on the existence of the enterprise. In turn, the enterprise depends on the continuation of a variety of services from the community and on the corporate "shield" against individual responsibility. Yet while capital has been quick to insist on a quid pro quo from workers, it has been slow to abide by such a mutual responsibility in relation to communities.

In manufacturing today, this understanding of the communal nature of work has been severely eroded. Wage costs are becoming increasingly important as capital and technology become universally available on comparable terms and as transportation and communication costs drop. Comparative advantage now goes to those countries whose industrial plant is newest and most efficient, but even more important, to those countries whose workers are often the lowest paid and least organized. The presence or absence of conventional natural resources or a level of development sufficient to create new technology is no longer a principal determinant of advantage.

As industry moves many of its labor-intensive activities to low-wage havens abroad, thereby evading U.S. health, safety, labor and environmental laws, it also devastates the communities left behind— eliminating jobs, markets, a viable tax base and the hope for a better future. Industries also frequently violate agreements with cities and counties under which they had received tax abatements and other benefits. Agreements, moreover, do not preclude their leaving the area altogether or substantially reducing the number of jobs. For example, the Louisiana Coalition for Tax Justice reported that from 1980 to 1989 the state provided more than $1.28 billion in tax giveaways to oil refining, paper and chemical industries, while over the same period those industries shed over 8,000 jobs.

If workers believe they must compete against each other in the new world economic order by accepting deeper and deeper wage and benefit cuts, such "progress" on a world scale will, perversely, have led us back to where we were in the United States before the establishment of the trade union movement. Already we are seeing signs of this regression: declining real wages; the growth of child labor; the return of a 10- and 12-hour day; and the erosion of hard won health and safety standards. Beyond this, unemployment is pervasive, homelessness is spreading, and social pathologies related to the destruction of viable communities and social networks are prevalent, including alcoholism and drug addiction, wife and child abuse, racist violence and violent crime.

Public Regulation of Private Capital

Without alternatives to this "standard" way of doing business, corporate abandonment will continue to devastate the communities of the United States and work to the detriment of most working people abroad. Indeed, according to the International Labour Organisation, unemployment and underemployment across the world is now at its highest level since the Great Depression. One out of three workers is either out of work or making too little to afford the basic necessities. The effects of such corporate hegemony must be increasingly counter-balanced by governmental action aimed at protecting the interests of working people and local communities.

The imposition of social limits on private capital is based on the great economic advantages that are granted to corporations by the public, including the limited personal liability of their stock and bond holders and management. Regaining public control over capital in a globalized economy is vital to the quest for economic justice and full employment. In particular, it is essential that investments made by the largest corporations, which control the major share of U.S. investment capital, contribute to achieving the desired goals of full employment at decent wages and environmental preservation.

The governments of Europe and Japan have been more willing to impose controls on capital than the government of the United States. Contrary to business assumptions, such controls do not necessarily stifle a country's productivity rates or competitive position. Productivity in Germany, for example, jumped 25 percent between 1980 and 1986 and investment per employee more than doubled between 1970 and 1986, despite the fact that layoffs and plant closings were more highly regulated than in the United States. Even in Europe, however, greater international trade competition is leading to pressures for reductions in controls and social welfare spending. Some intra-country regulation of the movement of industrial plants and other major sources of employment is needed in order to ensure adequate, stable regional and local investment. It may also be necessary to regulate the export of capital in order to ensure adequate national investment for full employment, preferably in concert with other industrial economies. Increasingly, we need to apply the principle of "full cost accounting" to capital movement, so that capital can move only after it has met the full social and environmental costs its moving creates, including past incentives and tax breaks from local and state governments.

Several policy initiatives should be undertaken to achieve community preservation and support. First, a company employing a significant number of workers within a community should be required to provide a community impact statement and to negotiate with the community if it wishes to reduce employment significantly. The purpose of both these requirements would be to agree on the amount of compensation needed to enable local community leaders to plan for the change. If necessary, the facility might be converted to an alternative purpose, using and/or retraining the company's work force. Business establishments should either *stay or pay*—either continue to provide productive employment, or pay a portion of the cost of the community's previous extension of roads, plumbing and schools for its workers and the cost of conversion to alternative uses that will generate income and employment.

Second, employers should not be given tax incentives to transfer their operations overseas. The U.S. tax code has rewarded U.S.-based multinationals that invest abroad rather than at home in two ways. The first way is to reward a company that invests overseas and pays taxes to a foreign government with preferential treatment in the form of a foreign tax credit. That is, the full amount of taxes that it pays to the foreign government is subtracted from the company's federal tax liability. By contrast, a company that pays the same amount in taxes to a state where it does business can only deduct the state tax from its federal taxable income. The result is that the company that stays at home will pay more in federal taxes than the company making a comparable income abroad. About two-thirds of this tax credit goes to manufacturing companies which are, in effect, rewarded for accelerating the erosion of the U.S. industrial job base.

The second way is with the foreign tax deferral privilege. U.S. corporations can avoid paying any federal income tax on earnings of their foreign subsidiaries, unless and until the profits are returned to the United States. This amounts to an interest-free loan from U.S. taxpayers for firms that wish to expand overseas by keeping their profits abroad, and in many cases results in outright immunity from U.S. taxes for profits that remain overseas.

Removing the privileged status of income earned abroad would not only make the tax system fairer. It would add an estimated $17.5 billion to federal tax revenues and would also end two of the government incentives to shift jobs overseas.

There are, in addition, other ways in which the United States government entices corporations to move overseas. Investigations by the National Labor Committee for Worker and Human Rights in Central

America and the Caribbean (a coalition of 23 national trade unions) have revealed that the Reagan and Bush administrations channeled more than $1 billion in tax dollars through the United States Agency for International Development (USAID) to build "export processing zones" in Central America and the Caribbean and to finance "investment promotion programs" (see also, Section 7, "Fair Trade and Economically viable Local Production for Local Consumption").

The USAID actively urged U.S. businesses to locate in these low-wage zones, which now house more than 3,000 plants that employ more than 735,000 workers and export more than $14 billion annually to the United States. The workers in these zones (who are disproportionately female) lack the most basic human rights, and are routinely subjected to physical, sexual, emotional and environmental abuse. If they attempt to organize they are fired and blacklisted and sometimes killed. Many zones are encircled with fences and razor wire and have armed guards at the gates. Instead of deploring such violations of human rights, the U.S. government has provided subsidized training, technical assistance and worker training programs for U.S. companies that move to these zones. Moreover, U.S. military assistance to the governments of these low-wage countries is often used to train and equip the military and police forces that brutally quell worker strikes and protest.

Influenced by a year-long investigation by the National Labor Committee, Congress passed an amendment to the FY 1992 Foreign Assistance Act prohibiting these practices. Nevertheless, U.S. taxpayer dollars continue to support such activities. Continued public pressure and strict monitoring are needed in order to enforce the new prohibitions.

Local Job and Economic Development

The United States needs a policy of promoting full employment through traditional macroeconomic policies but also through local job and economic development, with job training based upon local markets. Such policies, as in some European welfare states, should be designed to promote mobility without undermining individual and community well-being and security. A flexible network of local, regional, and national public development banks and public enterprises seems to be the most desirable structure for achieving this.

The new policy must ensure that public enterprises will be created where private enterprise is unable or unwilling to provide the goods, services and employment required by regions and communities. When companies leave or threaten to leave a community, public development banks can provide loans that will allow the plant to stay open, or be converted to some other productive activity. Also technical assistance is needed by communities and workers wishing to develop local markets and products for the local economy.

Community Federalism

This new policy should incorporate democratic planning processes (see Section 8, "Democratic Planning and Industrial Policy"), based upon principles which may be called "community federalism." In such a structure, local participation and control exist side-by-side with national and international regulatory and standard-setting mechanisms. Together they can insure that the program will meet the needs of working peoples and communities.

The community-federalist structure of planning and program implementation should begin at the community level, with community and regionally-selected bodies having the authority to prepare and implement economic development plans, including creating enterprises that will provide needed goods and services to their communities. Non-market criteria, such as local full employment, local provision of goods and services, environmental protection, affirmative action, pay equity, preservation of stable communities and the creation of humane work environments, are central to this design. Such criteria should be enforced by regulation and, more importantly, by incorporating these interests into the planning process.

5.

MILITARY CONVERSION

For decades, the military budget, driven by a military-industrial complex that President Dwight Eisenhower warned would lead to the rise of misplaced power, has eaten up a huge part of total federal expenditures. It has drained resources from civilian uses, diverted scientists from creating new civilian products and industries, fostered duplicative and wasteful procurement and production processes, increased the size of the federal deficit, distorted national and regional priorities and led to ecological destruction.

The Costs of the Military Economy

It is estimated that since the end of World War II, the U.S. has spent approximately $11 trillion on the military—an amount exceeding the money value of the nation's entire stock of civilian industrial plant, equipment and infrastructure. In recent years, military purchases alone have been around 78 percent of all federal government purchases. Estimates of the proportion of the federal budget going to the military range from 24 percent to 52 percent, depending on whether one includes that portion of the debt that pays for past wars as well as portions of the budgets of other departments that are military-related, such as the Department of Energy's huge weapons complex. At 5.2 percent of the GDP, direct outlays for the military in 1991 exceeded the percentage of GDP going to the military of all of our major economic competitors.

Between 30 and 60 percent of the nation's best scientific minds are employed in creating weapons of mass destruction—minds that could be better employed in designing new civilian technologies, such as environmentally sound transportation and energy systems or other infrastructure systems.

Two-thirds of all federal research and development money is invested in the military, compared with 5 and 15 percent respectively in Japan and Germany. Our neglect of civilian research and development has contributed to the loss of competitiveness among our civilian industries. Our decaying and neglected human and physical capital, too, have weakened our economy and society.

Rather than making us safer, military spending is making the world a more dangerous place. The international trade in arms—much of it fueled by U.S. weapons manufacturers—continues to create and exacerbate international instability and civil wars in dozens of nations across the globe, the Bush Administration's arming of Saddam Hussein being a case in point. The arms trade also undercuts the legal, rational and moral authority of the United Nations.

Claiming the Peace Dividend

With the end of the Cold War, the United States has an unprecedented opportunity to shift to a peacetime economy based on meeting human needs and fostering international cooperation. The United States has untold needs in health care, child care, elder care, education and other human services; there is an urgent need for rebuilding our cities and for developing a comprehensive housing program; for new and renovated water and sewage systems; for new and renovated mass transit systems; for road, bridge, tunnel and dam repair; for railroad electrification and for toxic waste cleanup. In short, there is no dearth of work that needs to be done.

When seen in historical perspective, the task of shifting from military to civilian production seems eminently feasible. After World War II, demobilization cut the military budget by 90 percent. The nation is still reaping the benefits from some of the programs this made possible, such as the GI Bill, which not only eased the transition but also enhanced the education of millions of Americans, thus contributing to U.S. economic progress in the postwar decades.

While former Secretary of Defense Les Aspin claimed that the 1994 Pentagon spending request was "in many ways the first truly post-Cold

War budget," the Pentagon failed to cancel any of the major weapons systems begun during the Cold War—a policy that could have saved $16 billion in one year and as much as $100 billion in future years. While President Clinton proposed to reduce military spending by $14 billion or 4.7 percent, the retired admirals and other top military personnel at the Center for Defense Information, hardly "doves," estimated that the United States could maintain the strongest military in the world, even after reducing annual military spending from the 1992 level of $291 billion to $200 billion in 1996, a reduction of nearly one third.

Many other experts believe that substantial cuts in the military budget can be made without jeopardizing national security. Estimates range from the Brookings Institution's cut of one-third over ten years to the Congressional Black Caucus' call for halving the military budget within four years. Former CIA director, William Colby, called for cutting military spending by 50 percent within five years. The Congressional Black Caucus' proposal is eminently reasonable, given the fact that at least half of the military budget has been allocated for the defense of Western Europe.

Any meaningful program to cut the military, however, must be linked to a strong program of investment in human and physical capital and must ease the transition for affected workers and communities. Considerable support for the military budget has always come from its ability to generate jobs. Thus, it is important to understand that military expenditures create fewer jobs than comparable civilian expenditures. Cuts in the military budget will not cause a net loss of jobs, if these funds are transferred to civilian uses. Indeed, if they are so transferred, even more jobs will be created.

Conversion Planning

Gains can come from cuts in the military budget but only if they are accompanied by careful conversion planning. Some of the new jobs may require skills similar to the old ones. But other new jobs may require different skills. Further, military bases and industries tend to be concentrated geographically, and many communities are highly dependent on one base or plant.

To facilitate conversion planning, an Office of Economic Conversion, accountable to the new Economic Security Council, should be set up. Conversion planning must insure adequate income security and offer adequate employment and/or education, training or retraining opportunities, and in some cases relocation assistance for civilian or military personnel who lose their jobs when bases are closed, plants shut down and the size of the armed forces reduced. Early retirement with no loss of pension benefits may also be an option for some.

We are cognizant of the possible impact of military downsizing on minorities, who are disproportionately employed by the military. Lack of opportunity in civilian employment has caused many minority youths to seek military careers. Their demobilization should not thrust them into unemployment, underemployment or poverty. Instead, there must be provision of adequate income security, employment and training opportunities that will insure a smooth transition to productive civilian lives *for all.*

During this transition period, the government must also offer economic planning grants to communities facing base and plant closings, and must assist small and medium-sized firms in developing non-military production. Incentives might be offered to defense companies that are willing to plan ahead for civilian conversion.

Priority in the use of the peace dividend ought to be given to meeting human needs and financing initiatives in areas like environmentally safe energy and transportation systems in which the market is initially unwilling to invest. Indeed, Transportation Secretary Frederico Pena has said that transportation technologies "are the most ripe for defense conversion," and he has encouraged increased federal financing of such technologies. With initial government support, such areas can yield productive new industries.

The Office of Economic Conversion would estimate the effect of cuts on regions, industries and population groups and advise the President and Congress on how best to handle the economic transformation. It could also publicize successful conversion experiments, as well as monitor and evaluate the results. We recommend that the Office of Economic Conversion consult with local alternative-use committees on which there would be equal representation of labor, management and the community.

The release of funds from the military to civilian uses offers our nation the opportunity to reinvest these resources in ways that will bring enhanced national security by reweaving the tattered economic and social fabric of society. But without meaningful conversion planning, mounting political pressure will prevent significant cuts in the military budget. President Clinton's disappointing promise of no more defense cuts in his 1994 State of the Union message reflects such pressures.

Even if these pressures are resisted, the voices of deficit reduction will continue to be heard. To use the peace dividend solely to reduce the federal deficit, as some have suggested, would, as Seymour Melman put it, be a sure route to a third-rate economy.

In addition to the implementation of a comprehensive conversion plan, we recommend that stronger measures be taken to develop international agreements to halt the spread of arms, including the enforcement of the Nuclear Non-Proliferation Treaty Implementation Act, and ratification of all pending treaties to cut nuclear and conventional weaponry. The unwillingness of the United States to curb the power of its own military-industrial complex has played a major role in the inability of the world's nations to end the weapon's scourge.

6.

ENVIRONMENTAL PRESERVATION

AND SUSTAINABILITY

Any full employment program must adhere to the principles of sustainable growth and development. Contrary to some environmentalists, who have called for zero-growth as the only way to preserve the planet, we believe that sustainability—the ability of the earth's systems to regenerate themselves for the use of future generations—is not incompatible with growth.

Defining Sustainable Growth and Development

The question that must be addressed is what kind of growth? Growth that uses up non-renewable resources at an accelerating rate and causes the destruction of critical ecosystems is not sustainable growth. There can, however, be growth in products and services that do not pollute, that actually reduce current levels of degradation and that help to regenerate the ecosystem. Converting from military production to highly efficient, non-polluting mass transit systems and from high-tech, invasive health care to preventive health care and education for more healthful lifestyles will reduce current levels of environmental destruction and improve the quality of life. Educating people to move from a high beef diet to a largely vegetarian diet, for example, will help to preserve many ecosystems now being destroyed by the cattle industry. "Greening" the inner cities to provide more space for parks, gardens and other recreational areas are forms of growth that will help to regenerate the urban environment. Service jobs that improve our quality of life, such as child and elder care, also do not degrade the environment. Thus, growth in social welfare expenditures is sustainable growth.

Sustainable development includes environmental costs and benefits in the development plan so that environmentally protective growth becomes economically desirable. Economic development consultant Michael Jacobs has argued that sustainable development should also distribute the creation and conservation of resources more fairly. This is necessary, not only because it is morally right, but because extremes of poverty and wealth are environmentally destructive. Great wealth enables its owners to displace the costs of their excessive consumption of environmentally destructive products and processes onto the less privileged so that the true consequences of such consumption are "out of sight, out of mind." Thus, the rich countries ship their most polluting technologies and products to "poor" countries, while enacting environmental regulations in their own. (Most of the industrialized nations, with the exception of the United States, signed a covenant in 1994 promising to end this practice.) For their part, the poor are often forced to use up the land and resources remaining to them in a non-sustainable fashion simply to survive. The overcrowded and dreadfully polluted shantytowns that ring the world's largest cities and the destruction of the forests of Africa, Asia and Latin America for firewood or cattle grazing are examples of the consequences of extreme poverty. Since unemployment and underemployment contribute to income disparities, especially in the absence of strong welfare state policies, international full employment becomes a necessary, though not sufficient, condition for sustainable development.

The Clinton Administration has taken some welcome first steps in the direction of sustainable development by creating a President's Council on Environmental Sustainability to create new approaches for combining economic development with environmental protection. It is also redirecting some of its foreign aid toward sustainable development projects and lobbying the World Bank toward the same end. The Administration is also moving to develop new rules to keep racial minorities and the poor from bearing the brunt of domestic environmental pollution and has signed the international Convention on Biological Diversity. However, the Administration's and Congress's fixation on the budget deficit, the weak environmental side agreements attached to the North American Free Trade Agreement (NAFTA), the failure of the Administration to sign the ban against toxic dumping as well as its failure to address the issue of income inequality in any significant way are likely to undermine these positive efforts.

Environmental Protection and Job Creation

Many people are beginning to realize that production that pollutes is actually counterproductive. For example, the Mount Sinai School of Medicine in New York has put a multibillion dollar price tag on the cost of toxic-related cancers. The California Toxics Coordinating Project estimates that lost worker productivity, crop loss and cleanup associated with the toxic economy amount to billions of dollars in California alone. When *all* the social and economic costs are counted, it is cheaper to produce the goods and services our society needs in a clean and sustainable way than it is to poison the earth and then use valuable resources to clean it up.

Environmental protection is therefore *good* for the economy and should be a central element in a program of job creation. Much new employment will be generated by the activities required for conversion to a sustainable economy. Some will produce new consumer products; others will modify production processes, making industry more efficient by reducing waste products and lowering material disposal costs. As Michael Renner points out, many of the industries needed in an environmentally sustainable economy will be far more labor intensive. We should convert, as rapidly as possible, to sustainable forms of goods and services production, including energy conservation and renewable energy sources. New industries and new jobs will be created, especially at the community level, where local enterprises and local development authorities can work together to create a new, environmentally-sound economy.

Much needs to be done to restrict the emissions from existing industries, to convert other industries to renewable forms of energy and material consumption and to clean up the residue from the environmental errors of the past. All of these entail "productive" work, not necessarily in the limited sense of producing more goods, but in the sense of producing a better life for all.

We should make more vigorous efforts to decrease our present dependence on fossil fuels. Not only is the burning of coal, oil and natural gas a principal cause of atmospheric pollution, acid rain and possible global warming, but these nonrenewable fuels are being depleted. By increasing the efficiency with which we use these fuels and by turning to renewable biological and solar energy sources, we will create new sources of employment and retard the depletion of these increasingly scarce resources.

We recommend the expansion of recycling and the reuse of secondary materials. While this part of the economy has been marginal until now, it should become a central feature of production and consumption in all industrialized countries. New opportunities abound in this field, especially for community-based enterprises. Like some other industries that perform important work, the recycling industry currently pays low wages, so it is important that wages and working conditions in this and other low-wage but useful industries be substantially upgraded through unionization and the salutary effects of full employment.

Public Policy Support for Environmental Sustainability

The shift to a sustainable economy such as we have described will not happen without a supporting public policy—one that recognizes the full social and environmental costs of goods and processes that pollute and use nonrenewable resources. The current use of the GDP to measure a nation's growth and well-being is totally inadequate to the task of shaping a sustainable economy. Such measures exclude the long-term costs to health and the environment of polluting and environmentally destructive products and production processes. They also count as income many of the expenditures needed to clean up pollution and its adverse consequences. In order to make prices more realistic for polluting goods, such currently ignored costs as the risks of global warming, the expense of military units considered necessary to assure access to Middle East oil, health and disposal costs of toxics, and all the other spillover costs currently excluded from private cost accounting must be factored in. This will require a fundamental restructuring of the rules and practices that shape economic decisionmaking.

To this end we call on the President's Council of Economic Advisers to work with the President's new Council on Environmental Sustainability to develop a social and environmental accounting process. Such accounts would include all of the currently excluded variables that could impact on the government's fiscal policies and would adjust the measures of costs and benefits so that real benefits could be distinguished from illusory gains. Several models of such "social and environmental accounting" processes are already available. The United Nations Statistical Commission now provides guidelines for incorporating environmental damages into national accounting procedures.

The Worldwatch Institute has suggested the development of a green tax code that, if phased in gradually, would reshape fiscal policy by taxing the use of nonrenewable and polluting resources and processes. This, in turn, would provide an incentive for businesses to move toward more sustainable forms of production. It is possible that the taxes of other businesses that adhere to green policies could be lowered. Discussion of such green tax codes has already been on the agenda of the European Union (EU, formerly the European Community).

Public policy can also generate guaranteed markets for solar energy or recycled materials (as it did for military equipment and computers) through its subsidies to private industry as well as through its procurement policies. Currently, federal energy subsidies go disproportionately to fossil fuels (58 percent) and nuclear energy (30 percent), while only 3 percent support energy efficiency and 2 percent support renewable sources. Such funding priorities should be reversed. We are encouraged by the Clinton Administration's decision to purchase lower fuel emission cars for its fleet. Much more can be done, however, not only by the federal government, but also by state and local governments. California, for example, has committed 40 percent of its procurement budget to recycled products by 1995, while Connecticut has required that by 1995 telephone directories contain 30 percent recycled paper. The government should also fund research to replace nonrenewable with renewable resources. In order to do this, it should shift a greater amount of R & D money from military to civilian research projects.

Planning for Conversion to an Environmentally Sustainable Economy

As industry, under the force of stricter environmental limits, shifts from a hard energy path (fossil fuel and nuclear energy) to a soft one (renewable sources, conservation), many jobs related to the oil, coal and atomic industries will be lost. In the long run, the transition from high-tech, capital intensive energy use to less capital intensive, decentralized, energy conserving industries is likely to produce more jobs. But workers displaced from polluting industries that are declining may not have the requisite skills or live where the jobs are expanding. Comprehensive programs similar to those proposed for military conversion (see Section 5, "Military Conversion") are needed to ease the transition of affected workers and communities. For workers, these include, but are not limited to, free retraining with adequate income support (see Section 11, "Lifelong Learning") and relocation allowances, if needed.

But the bottom line is guaranteed jobs at adequate wages. Without such a guarantee, these workers and communities will resist efforts to create an environmentally sound economy for fear of becoming endangered species or ghost towns. And employers will continue to violate environmental standards by threatening workers and communities with job loss. Workers and communities should not have to trade hazardous health conditions and environmental degradation for jobs. Only a JOBS FOR ALL program such as we are proposing would make it possible for workers and their communities to resist what Richard L. Grossman and Richard Kazis have called "job blackmail."

7.

FAIR TRADE AND ECONOMICALLY VIABLE LOCAL PRODUCTION FOR LOCAL CONSUMPTION

The corporate-driven globalization of the economy—facilitated by declining costs and advances in transportation and communication—is the most obvious economic phenomenon of the present period. Capital is much more mobile than labor, and in a world economy in which wages, working conditions, and environmental rules vary enormously, firms locate where their production costs are lowest. Under conditions of chronic world underemployment the global mobility of corporations permits them to negotiate even lower costs and standards.

Multinational interests have accelerated the process of globalization by pressing for global trade and investment agreements which improve their access to markets, protect their profits and minimize interference from local governments. These agreements have been negotiated under the auspices of the General Agreement on Tariffs and Trade (GATT), most recently the Uruguay Round, completed December 15, 1993. (Future agreements will be made under the newly formed World Trade Organization.) Earlier GATT rounds steadily reduced barriers to trade, but the Uruguay Round has extended rules to new areas, such as limits on what governments can do to encourage locally-owned industry.

There have been regional agreements as well, NAFTA and the EU being the most important. These agreements have in common the enlargement and protection of returns to capital ownership. While enforceable international rules now protect property rights and enhance the bargaining power of corporations, there are no comparable protections for workers. Though far from perfect, the EU, unlike NAFTA, does have a Social Charter.

The argument for lowering trade and investment barriers is that producing where costs are relatively lowest will lead to maximum world output. Increasing output, however, will not necessarily improve the distribution of goods and services or lead to higher wages. It is worth noting that the decline in the standard of living for the average American coincides with the accelerating integration of the United States into the world economy. Though this coincidence is not conclusive evidence of the malign effects of international competition on wages, it at least challenges the happy conclusion that most people will obviously benefit from freer trade and investment.

Global Regulation of Demand, Corporations and the Environment

Increased global production will not lead to increased aggregate demand unless it is accompanied by publicly regulated global demand management (see also, Section 4, "Community Investment, Preservation and Support"). Currently, international agencies such as the International Monetary Fund are forcing indebted countries to decrease their spending. The power of national governments to control what happens within their borders has been diminished by integration. The nation with a fiscal or monetary policy which is relatively expansive risks trade deficits with slower growing economies and consequently currency depreciation, as financial interests transfer their funds to achieve higher interest rates. Unregulated and untaxed financial flows, mostly speculative, are another impediment to global demand management and should be governed by international rules.

The international community also needs to set universal operating rules on multinational businesses so that they cannot use their considerable bargaining power to negotiate concessions from a poor country as a condition for their investments. Their current powers vis-a-vis governments have been enhanced by the latest GATT agreement as well as by NAFTA.

The recent global agreements have not adequately considered the environmental consequences of expanded international competition and economic growth. President Clinton, an enthusiastic supporter of the recent GATT agreement, afterwards suggested that the next round of GATT talks should consider the environment, labor standards and antitrust policies. Labor, the environment, and economic power are too important to be afterthoughts.

Increasing world demand will mean increasing depletion of the earth's resources and environmental degradation if world output is expanded along the lines of the current development model. At the least, producers who meet domestic environmental regulations should be protected from international competitors who produce by more polluting methods (see Section 6, "Environmental Sustainability"). Many environmentalists have proposed social tariffs, which would add a tax to foreign goods so that their prices would reflect all social costs, meaning generally acceptable environmental and labor standards. Under the current GATT agreement, the generally more stringent U.S. environmental laws which keep out foreign goods not meeting U.S. standards can be challenged as trade barriers. Similarly, the European ban on U.S. meat containing growth hormones can be challenged as a nontariff barrier to trade.

The basis for international trade should be the principle of non-exploitative exchange relations, including support for equitable wages, decent working conditions (including workers' health and safety) and protection of the environment. The goal of trade agreements should not be the extractive benefits that flow to a few through so-called "free trade," but the benefits that would flow to all through fair and equal trade; agreements should also aim to maximize democratic control and mutually supportive relations among the world's working people.

The new World Trade Organization (WTO), which is proposed as a replacement for the GATT, will not be based on these principles unless there is a outcry from the ordinary people whose lives and livelihoods will be affected by it. According to Ralph Nader, as currently proposed, the WTO would be run by unelected bureaucrats in Geneva, Switzerland, away from the control of the elected representatives of the nations whose economies will be affected. The WTO would have the power to declare national, state or local laws that seek to protect worker and consumer rights or the environment as nontariff barriers to trade and therefore null and void. In order to defend any of these laws, a U.S. trade official would have to travel to Geneva to make the case before a three-person trade tribunal in a proceeding whose records would be kept secret from the press, from elected officials and from the public.

Local Production for Local Consumption

Sometimes it may be beneficial to encourage local production for local consumption (see also Section 4, "Community Investment, Preservation and Support"). Such production tends to conserve energy and reduce environmental pressures by, for example, lessening the need for transportation. It makes no sense for Southeast Asia to import rice from the United States. Nor, for that matter, does it make sense for the "garden state" of New Jersey to import tomatoes from California in the summer. Sometimes, however, there are real efficiencies to be gained through trade because of economies of scale and different natural endowments. No community can be expected to make or grow every product it uses; nor can every nation. Large as it is, the United States mainland grows no coffee. But if trade is to be beneficial rather than harmful to ordinary people, it must be based on the principles mentioned. And, when costs and efficiencies are considered in determining the viability of a particular strategy, the distributional impact must be factored in, as well as all costs—including social ones. If local production for local consumption were to be given greater emphasis, local economies might discover new uses for natural resources that are now useless; and countries whose populations are oriented toward a few export commodities utilizing a limited range of technologies would be encouraged to develop more diversified economies.

International Policy and Developing Countries

Trade and foreign investment alone do not spell a genuine development strategy. Such a strategy would have broadly rising living standards as its major target, especially for the poorest people in these countries. Some appropriate policies would include debt relief, greater control of multinational firms, a shift toward sustainable production and resource use in rich countries, and a gradual upward harmonization and enforcement of labor and environmental standards. The point is to raise standards and incomes in poorer countries, rather than to lower those in richer ones.

NAFTA includes Canada as well as Mexico, where wages are one-tenth those in the United States. NAFTA is an example of a trade agreement that is not geared to upward harmonization. Hence, it will not necessarily benefit many Mexican workers, especially the poorest, even as it threatens living standards of U.S. workers.

Experience from the maquiladora program is instructive though not encouraging. Even before NAFTA, hundreds of thousands of U.S. jobs had fled to Mexico under that program, an arrangement enabling U.S. owned plants to operate along the border inside Mexico, and then to export their wares back to the United States with little or no tariffs. Lured by low wages and the ability to evade U.S. labor and environmental standards, many maquiladoras pay Mexicans bare subsistence wages and generate air pollution and toxic wastes that rank among the world's worst. Though they work in modern plants, maquiladora workers often live without running water, electricity or sewers; home may be a dormitory or a shack made from packing materials.

Although tariff barriers between Mexico and the United States were already low on many items, large numbers of Mexicans have not benefited. Nor have they benefited since that country began opening its economy to extensive trade in the early 1980s. As for those on the bottom, conditions have worsened. Between 1976 and 1990, the real minimum wage in Mexico declined by 60 percent. Also, increasing orientation toward foreign trade has destroyed Mexico's self-sufficiency in food. The extensive importation of grain has pushed many small farmers off the land and into the ranks of the urban unemployed— and some of them into the ranks of illegal immigrants to the United States. NAFTA is expected to decimate much of Mexico's traditional corn economy and has already led to protests by indigenous people in the province of Chiapas. Not only is this tragic for Mexican farmers, but scientists fear that if the Mexican corn economy is destroyed by American imports, a vast genetic stock of hundreds of varieties will be lost to humankind. Genetic diversity is increasingly recognized as essential to the preservation of the ecosphere and to the supply of food for human beings.

NAFTA will accelerate the flight of U.S. capital—especially for long-term investment—and hence of jobs, to Mexico, now that fear of future expropriation has been allayed by making investment safe for U.S. corporations. Although NAFTA insures the property rights of these investors through its status as an international treaty, it makes no mention of human rights. And it poses a grave threat to U.S. labor and environmental standards. Nor do the impotent side agreements on labor and the environment alter this fact. This is unlike action of the EU. When it planned to include poorer European countries, it negotiated a Social Charter to raise their workplace standards and minimum wage levels.

. Although the EU Social Charter also requires maintenance of democratic institutions, NAFTA contains no similar requirement and weakens the possibility of democratization in Mexico as well as representative government in the United States. Mexico's one-party system does not nurture independent institutions; watchdog organizations like Amnesty International and America's Watch report extensive human rights violations. Professor Adolfo Aguilar Zinser of Mexico's National University, also President of the Lazaro Cardenas Foundation, warns that without democratic reform, NAFTA will "only invigorate the power of the few, deepen social inequities, and invigorate despotism." In the United States, where elected representatives still have some accountability to the people, NAFTA takes crucial economic decisions out of their hands and puts them in the hands of unelected, totally unaccountable groups whose interests lie in the maximization of private profit.

Implications of "Free Trade" for U.S. Workers and Public Policy

Estimates of the net employment impact of these international agreements vary widely. In the case of NAFTA, for example, proponents claim many benefits for U.S. workers. Ironically, many of these claims are based on flawed studies that assume there will be full employment in the United States. But even some of NAFTA's proponents acknowledge there will be some job loss. Lynn Martin, Secretary of Labor in the Bush Administration, admitted a potential loss of 150,000 U.S. jobs. Jeff Faux and Thea Lee of the Economic Policy Institute, however, estimate an eventual loss of from 290,000 to 550,000 jobs—and downward pressure on the wages of 70 percent of U.S. workers. By placing continuous pressure on U.S. workers to lower wages and standards, NAFTA will be encouraging many U.S. producers to respond to international competition with technological stagnation and low wages rather than with productivity improvement, innovation and high-wages.

It is also important to recognize that, even if there were to be no *net* loss of jobs, NAFTA will still impact negatively on the employment and wages of large numbers of American workers. Indeed, as a study of the Joint Economic Committee of Congress points out, such a scenario could occur "even if the United States turned out to be a marginal winner in net jobs." An increase in employment for computer professionals, for example, will not offset the loss of jobs by garment workers. And in a stagnant labor market with desperate jobless workers, downward pressure on wages and standards will affect many workers who do not lose their jobs. A firm does not even have to move any of its operations abroad to wring concessions from its workers. A threat to move where wages are lower will do! While some may gain, negative employment and wage impacts will be especially pronounced among minorities, unskilled blue-collar workers and those without a college education—the very groups which have already suffered declining wages and disproportionately high unemployment.

Support is sorely needed for generous transitional assistance for U.S. workers, industries and communities negatively impacted by international agreements and the globalization of production. Experience with the Trade Adjustment Assistance program, however, makes us wary. As the U.S. Department of Labor has documented, retrained workers often cannot find jobs and relatively few are reemployed at suitable wages. For these programs to work, they must be part of a genuine full employment strategy with guaranteed jobs. Only such a program can allay the legitimate fears of workers and their communities that they are or will be victims of downward harmonization. Thus we invite all, even those who feel these fears are unjustified, to support a program of JOBS FOR ALL.

As we have shown, international trade agreements are not the only arenas for change. In addition to the aforementioned policies, government should target incentives such as loan guarantees and tax concessions to enterprises that will encourage local community development and broad participation in decision-making. Support for international financial agencies like the World Bank and the International Monetary Fund must also be conditioned on their commitment to the principles of workers' rights, enhancement of the quality of life, environmental sustainability and encouragement of viable local production for local consumption.

8.

DEMOCRATIC PLANNING
AND INDUSTRIAL POLICY

Full employment will require some coordination of public and private economic policy. Contrary to conventional wisdom, the United States has long been engaged in economic planning. We have had corporate planning for private profit and public/private planning for a war economy.

In the 1980s, profligate and unproductive private investment was coupled with cuts in public investment, with the exception of the military. Poor growth rates and a large federal deficit are the legacy of that kind of planning. Today, a huge backlog of needs—for affordable housing, mass transit, renewable energy, sound infrastructure, day care and preventive health care—go unmet. At the same time, we waste billions of dollars on weapons of mass destruction.

The time is overdue for a peace economy—one that sets the goals of economic justice and environmental sustainability and seeks to achieve these ends through democratic processes. If coupled with a commitment to local production for local consumption, democratic planning and coordination would ensure that goods and services are produced according to a more rational assessment of needs and demands.

Planning for such goals need not mean surrendering to a blueprint for "growth" drawn up by a highly centralized bureaucracy. Neither does it mean the production of goods and services for which there is no demand, nor the stifling of innovation and entrepreneurship.

Mechanisms for Planning

Planning, as we have envisioned it, would be carried out at local, regional and national levels, involving the ideas, skills, insights and concerns of many people. At the federal level, we suggest a National Economic Coordinating Council, composed of representatives of business, labor, government and the general public, with staff experts drawn from each of these constituencies. The Council should also be representative of the various geographical regions, ethnic and gender groups that make up the American polity. The Council, informed by local and regional bodies of similar composition, would work to assure the maximum development and utilization of the nation's human resources and the renewal of its productive capacities. Local and regional coordinating councils could encourage innovation and entrepreneurship with the expectation that if a product, process or service were successful, it could be institutionalized elsewhere.

Currently, this work is spread among several Cabinet departments, each of which competes for scarce resources and political attention. The result is waste, conflicting policies and the mismanagement of our productive capacity, as well as a federal bureaucracy susceptible to corporate manipulation. Bureaucratic fragmentation aids only those interest groups that have the financial resources to maintain a constant presence in Washington. The kind of coordinating body we suggest would obviate both the planning of a highly remote and centralized bureaucracy and the short-sightedness of corporate planning that is driven by short-term profit-making.

Fundamental to the success of such a coordinating council is the recognition by business, labor and government officials of the need to conclude a social compact. Such a compact would cover wages, executive pay, prices, rents, profits, dividends, interest and other income which would assure that all sectors share the gains and bear the burdens in some equitable way. The functions of such a coordinating body would be to:

- define and reconcile alternative needs and goals for private and public investment;

- encourage the kinds of technologies which are likely to support these objectives and discourage technologies that do not;

- determine and acquire the economic data needed for effective planning at the state level;

- nurture sustainable development;

- develop priorities for public and private action;

- create a public budget which reflects these priorities and their underlying values;

A Sound Industrial Policy

Implicit in the work of such a national coordinating body would be the development of a sound industrial policy for the nation. An industrial policy would help to integrate national economic policies and to coordinate federal, state and local government taxing and spending policies, national trade policies, and education and training policies. It would stimulate both public and private investment, including assistance where plant closings or economic conversion are taking place. It would also help to assure a healthy mix of both industrial and service enterprises.

By "healthy," we mean a mix of types of production and services that are able to develop and use the diverse interests and talents of the nation's workforce, as well as meet the real needs of the human community. The current emphasis on high-tech information processing and biotechnology is, we feel, misguided. There are some technologies which, because of the danger they pose to human health or the environment, should never be developed even if we have the capacity to develop them. Moreover, much of the world's population cannot use high-definition television or a supercomputer that can calculate more than a trillion mathematical operations each second. There is, however, a vast market for low and intermediate technologies to help the world's people house themselves, grow adequate food supplies, conserve potable water sources and develop renewable energy supplies. Industrial policy, based upon a sound and informed assessment of national, regional and local needs is not a matter of the government's choosing "winners" and "losers." Rather, it is assisting enterprises and industries in the making of products for which there is a significant public need.

Americans For Democratic Action (ADA) has suggested that one logical component of an industrial policy would be a National Civilian Technology Administration, patterned after the Defense Department's Advanced Research Projects Agency (DARPA).

In addition, an Industrial Extension Service, patterned after the Agricultural Extension Service, could provide assistance to both businesses and community groups. The Extension Service would aid businesses which need to modernize or find new product lines in order to create or preserve secure, well-paid jobs and it would also assist worker and community groups seeking to convert aging or abandoned industrial sites to new uses. Firms receiving such public help would be required to adhere to high product quality standards and to achieve environmental quality, workplace fairness and other important social and economic goals.

9.

REBUILDING THE NATION'S

CITIES

Unemployment not only has differential racial and gender impacts, but differential regional impacts as well. While the proposals made in other sections of this paper would benefit everyone, certain groups need to be addressed with special programs. A special category of funding should be targeted, for example, at the inner cities. This is necessary because of the strategic function of the cities for the national economy and because of the enormous deterioration of both their human and physical resources over the last two decades. While concentrating here on the inner cities, we are cognizant that many who live in rural areas, for example, farmworkers, displaced or engangered family farmers, Native Americans, Appalachians, and others will require a variety of special programs beyond what we have proposed. We recommend that subcommittees of our proposed Commission to Study and Propose Solutions to the Problems of Unemployment and Underemployment should take up the special problems of these groups (see Section 1, "Jobs for All").

Cities have historically been the heart of the nation. The financial, productive and cultural networks housed in cities have pumped the life blood that circulates throughout the entire economy. The knowledge that the health of a nation is dependent on its cities, however, seems to have eluded our policymakers who have allowed, and in many cases even encouraged, the development of urban blight and social pathology. Examples of policies that have encouraged urban decay include: the interstate highway system, that first led to white flight from the cities and then to job flight; the urban renewal policies of the 1950s and 1960s, which replaced vibrant downtown working-class neighborhoods with upscale office towers and convention centers; discriminatory mortgage policies of the Federal Housing Authority and the Veteran's Administration that supported segregated suburban housing; tax breaks and government subsidies that enabled companies to relocate to cheaper labor zones abroad; the defunding of community development corporations; and bank regulations that allowed the deposits from poor communities to be invested elsewhere.

Across the United States our older cities are in crisis. With their middle-class tax bases having long since fled to the suburbs and many manufacturing jobs having moved to other domestic and foreign locations, the older cities are home to some of the most marginalized people in the nation; and their neighborhoods are among the most polluted. In the high-poverty areas of the 100 largest cities as much as 40 percent of the population live below the official poverty line. Pockets of our central cities outrival parts of the Third World in the level of human degradation. The infant mortality rate in central Harlem, for example, is higher than it is in Bangladesh, and the adult longevity rate is lower.

Financing the Cities

Central city poverty calls for higher levels of services and taxes even as a city's ability to meet these demands is reduced. Concentrated poverty diminishes the quality of life, while higher taxes and social problems constrain economic growth, making many cities less desirable places in which to live and do business.

Even though urban poverty is caused by large economic and demographic changes that affect the entire nation, urban governments bear the brunt of their costs. The financing of cities has become a Catch 22. Over the last two decades, as federal aid to cities has been cut, mayors have been forced to grant enormous tax concessions to businesses in order to entice them to stay in the city to provide jobs, largely for the city's dwindling middle class. This means lower tax revenues to pay for essential services. And each such cutback compounds the social pathologies of the inner city, driving businesses out and increasing the need for more police, prisons and shelters for the homeless than would have been needed had jobs, housing and social services been provided in the first place. This expensive "management" of the poor, which is increasingly funded by state tax revenues and regulated by nonelected financial authorities, is turning the older cities into regional "poor-houses" and eroding the principle of home rule. It is a vicious circle, which social policy must address.

Unfortunately, as the Milton S. Eisenhower Foundation recently put it in its report on urban poverty, American cities are suffering "not just the failure of spending, but the failure of imagination." About the only idea that seems to have caught the imagination of Washington is the "urban enterprise zone," now slightly modified as the Clinton Administration's "empowerment zone." Whatever the name of the zones, they are, as critics have pointed out, a geographic version of trickle-down economics, for they assist business owners more than the poor.

One of the major fears raised by those who oppose massive job creation programs is that of inflation (see Section 1, "Jobs for All"). The inflationary consequences of increased government spending can be limited by targeting the spending to those activities that will most directly create *new* employment for the jobless. Tax cuts or general increases in spending tend to spread the additional funds into sectors where employment is already high, not just into underemployed sectors, thereby generating new inflationary pressures. If, instead, the spending is concentrated in those areas, such as the inner city, where unemployment is high, and job-training funds are focused on those individuals whose current lack of skills is keeping them out of the labor market, the inflationary effects will be minimized. What in Europe is called an "active labor market policy"—assisting workers in gaining the necessary skills and then moving them into the jobs that are created—can aid this non-inflationary growth process (see Section 1, "Jobs for All"). Thus, targeting job training, education and job creation at inner city poverty is good economics as well as good ethics.

Many individuals and groups in our society have called for concentrated national efforts to rebuild the nation's cities. Senator Bill Bradley (NJ) has proposed a package of six bills that would spend $1.44 billion a year to replicate successful grassroots initiatives. The National Conference of Mayors has presented the Clinton Administration with a package of 7,000 ready-to-go construction projects that would cost $27 billion and create 400,000 jobs. The Congressional Black Caucus has proposed spending $31 billion on the cities; and the National Urban League has called for an urban "Marshall Plan" costing $50 billion per year for a ten-year period. Given the mounting deterioration of the cities, the Urban League's figure of $50 billion a year does not seem unreasonable.

In our cities are countless jobs that need doing, such as low-income housing construction and rehabilitation, school construction and repair, pollution cleanup, environmental conservation and the "greening" of the city, park and museum maintenance, infrastructure repair, day care, teaching and health and human services of all kinds. The unemployed of the inner city are the potential workers for such jobs. Each unemployed or underemployed inner city resident who is currently a drain on the city's and nation's treasuries could become a contributing taxpayer if put to work doing important jobs such as these; and each could contribute to the solution of an urgent urban problem. In survey after survey, the inner city poor indicate that what they most want are jobs at decent wages. Because of what William Julius Wilson and Loic Wacquant have called the "transformation of the social and institutional structure of the inner city," a significant portion of national jobs and training programs must be targeted on the poorest areas (where poverty levels exceed 40 percent) in the 100 largest cities. A progressive plan for the cities should address six critical needs: jobs, education and training, affordable housing, the development of equity in homes and businesses, affordable health care and community control. In this program, we address ourselves specifically to the first three.

All these proposals recognize that while the older cities may currently be a drain on the economy, they could become the engine of national economic recovery. One benefit from rebuilding cities would be increased tourism. Cleaner, safer, more beautiful cities are ones that find themselves on travel itineraries, thereby attracting outside money, both domestic and foreign. The money that is spent on preserving and developing a city like Paris is an enormous investment, not only in a nation's history and spirit, but in its treasury as well. A revitalization program that includes historic preservation and other travel attractions can generate revenues for American cities.

An Integrated Policy Response to Urban Poverty

Since the poor in these areas suffer from a multitude of interlocking deprivations, programs providing an integrated set of policy responses will be required. It is not enough to provide education and job training without guaranteeing jobs that pay antipoverty wages, adequate transportation to get to the jobs, day care for working parents, drug and other rehabilitation services and affordable health care and housing. Fortunately, most of the services that poor people need in order to become more productive citizens require the creation of jobs for other poor people.

However, the machinery to develop an integrated approach to job creation and community development is lacking. Poor people's needs are currently addressed by at least five different Cabinet departments. Consequently, we suggest that the National Economic Coordinating Council establish a Task Force on Rebuilding the Nation's Cities. The purpose of the Task Force would be to develop a comprehensive program to rebuild the inner cities, drawing on the knowledge of what we know works, examples of which are available around the country and even abroad. World Hunger Year, for example, has been collecting case studies of successful grassroots community development projects around the country, and the Megacities Project of New York University has been collecting such data from cities around the world. The Task Force on Rebuilding the Nation's Cities would work with the departments of Housing and Urban Development, Health and Human Services, Education, Labor and others to assure that programs and services are integrated and coordinated. Wherever possible, decisions on which projects to fund and on their location should be made by local community development councils made up of representatives of local organizations with proven records of community trust and support in the delivery of successful and cost-effective community services.

Many of the strategies described elsewhere in this program could be utilized by the Task Force. For example, community development banks could be set up in each of the targeted cities to finance community development projects and to reinvest in the community. Other strategies, however, would have to be developed to meet the special needs of the urban poor.

An Urban Youth Conservation Corps

Programs targeted specifically at the education, training and job placement of low-income youth are crucial, as an entire generation is growing up without the social skills, training or education needed for productive participation in the labor force. Many of these youth are the foot soldiers in the massive drug war that is poisoning urban America. An emphasis on youth is not only an ethical priority, but a practical one if we are to insure a big enough pool of future contributions to the Social Security Trust Fund.

One suggestion that we find promising is the creation of an Urban Youth Conservation Corps, modeled after the Civilian Conservation Corps of the New Deal. In the process of development as a local program by a coalition of churches in the South Bronx (New York City), the Youth Conservation Corps would involve young people who are "at risk"—that is, who are unemployed, school drop-outs, drug addicted or unwed parents—in an intensive three-year program that would move them from a highly structured experience outside the city back into the neighborhoods from which they came. There they would engage in a period of education, job and parent training, drug rehabilitation (if needed) and work in community renovation projects. After that they would move on either to college, apprenticeship programs or guaranteed jobs. While expensive at first, such a program would pay for itself in the long run through savings in the costs of incarceration, an overburdened court system, welfare and other entitlement programs.

Jobs and Housing: Keys to Urban Development

The Low Income Housing Crisis Continues is the subtitle of the Center on Budget and Policy Priorities' second (1991) report on the subject in two years. In that document, Edward Lazere and his colleagues reveal that:

- In 1970, there were 6.8 million low cost rental units (defined as those costing less than $250 a month for rent and utilities in 1989 dollars, or 30 percent of a $10,000 annual income, which was below the poverty level for a three-person family). These 6.8 million units *exceeded* the number of low-income renters by 400,000.

- By 1983, there were 5.9 million low-cost units and 9.7 million low-income renters, a *shortage* of 3.8 million units.

- Between 1983 and 1989, the number of low-income renters remained the same, but the number of low-rent units declined still further, to 5.5 million.

- In 1989, some 18 percent of all poor households were living in units that were moderately or severely overcrowded or deficient.

- Over one-half (56 percent) of all poor white, black and Hispanic families spent 50 percent of their incomes or more on housing costs.

The number of persons who are "shelter poor" or forced to neglect other vital needs, such as food and clothing, was 27 million in the middle 1980s, according to the Joint Housing Center of the Massachusetts Institute of Technology. It goes without saying that "shelter poor" and vulnerability to homelessness are synonymous.

A big part of the housing problem is declining government support for low-income housing. From fiscal years 1977 through 1980, the Department of Housing and Urban Development (HUD) made commitments to provide rental assistance to an average of 290,000 additional low-income households each year. For the next decade, however, the figure dropped to an average of 78,000 a year, a shocking reduction of nearly three fourths— this, while the numbers of the poor were increasing. Henry Cisneros, HUD Secretary, has recently called homelessness a "structural problem in America: chronic, continuous, large scale and complex." We are encouraged by the fact that an interagency group requested by the Clinton Administration to draft a plan to end homelessness has finally recognized the scope of the problem. In keeping with what homeless advocates have been claiming for years, the draft plan estimates the number of the nation's homeless to have been as many as seven million at some point in the 1980s. We are concerned, however, that Congress's fixation on deficit reduction will make it virtually impossible to respond to the draft plan's call for action on this critical issue.

While our discussion here focuses on the urban housing crisis, we are mindful of rural problems similarly abetted by substantial cuts in the rural housing programs of the Farmers Home Administration. Indeed, the housing crisis in many areas of the country is by no means confined to urban areas. In suburban Nassau County, New York, for example, prices of housing have escalated to the extent that many children of residents are unable to settle there, thus weakening family life. Moreover, in many suburbs those providing vital services to the community cannot afford to reside where they are employed.

In the United States there is no entitlement to housing assistance for persons of poor or moderate means. In 1992, only one-fifth of the poor (18.4 percent) and 4.2 percent of the population as a whole lived in public or subsidized housing. By contrast, housing subsidies are entitlements in some other countries; everyone who qualifies by reason of income deficiency gets a housing subsidy. In the United States, there is a housing entitlement of a different kind. It consists of tax deductions on mortgage interest and property taxes for owner-occupied homes—a form of welfare that overwhelmingly benefits the better-off. In 1993, mortgage deductions alone cost the federal treasury $41 billion, 85 percent of which went to the most affluent quarter of the American population. In that same year, subsidies for low-income housing came to only $8.7 billion.

Creative government would have taken the opportunity to solve two pressing problems: the decline in affordable housing and the shortage of jobs at decent pay. Government expenditures for housing are a boon to the economy quite apart from the shelter they provide. Housing creates jobs in the very areas where the jobless reside, although it also draws on a much larger radius for the myriad of materials that are required. According to the Office of Employment Projections of the Bureau of Labor Statistics, an expenditure of $1 billion on multi-family housing in 1990 would have generated 26,225 jobs. An outlay of $16 billion, equivalent to the amount that could be saved from discontinuing some unneeded Cold War weapons, would create about 400,000 jobs.

New housing is more efficient than older housing, friendlier to the environment in its use of smaller amounts of fossil fuels, for example. Compared to highway construction, which encourages the use of automobiles, funds spent on housing can be far more conducive to a sustainable economy especially if built in conjunction with environmental planning. Monies used to renovate, including retrofit, older housing, are particularly compatible with environmental sustainability. As Jeremy Rifkin has written: "Nothing could be more important to developing a sustainable society and reestablishing a sense of meaning in our communities than providing adequate housing for millions of Americans who live in substandard conditions, or are homeless."

Rifkin points out that in the past decade, more than 2,000 grassroots organizations, including tenant associations, unions, community development corporations and churches, have come together on the local level to renovate and develop nearly 320,000 housing units, creating many permanent jobs. We agree with housing experts, Peter Dreier and John Atlas, that only the federal government has the power and resources to address the nation's housing needs. And we also endorse their views that, along with a national housing policy that provides adequate resources and standards and that targets funds for the most needy, we should give grassroots groups like local tenant organizations, community-based non-profit developers and advocates for the homeless the flexibility to design housing policies and programs that reflect local needs.

A congressional initiative that links job creation and affordable housing is the Jesse Gray Housing Bill of 1993 (HR 1380), introduced by Representative John Conyers, Jr. (MI), with 10 co-sponsors. HR 1380 calls for the construction of 500,000 public housing units and the revitalization of 100,000 more over the next 10 years. For the construction and revitalization of units under their jurisdictions, local public housing authorities would be required to carry out programs of job training and employment of individuals residing in the area, with priorities given to residents of public housing.

Health Care Reform: A Potential Job Generator

The health care reform program currently being discussed in Washington may result in the short-term displacement of health care workers. Many jobs may be lost if we eliminate much of the paperwork of the present system and move toward a less high-tech, less hospital-centered program. These jobs are held by people who can least afford to lose them—single mothers, minorities and older workers—that is, people who would have a very hard time making the transition to another career. In this case, special provisions for retraining and reemployment should be made, such as those proposed for the retraining of other displaced workers (see Section 5, "Military Conversion"; Section 6, "Environmental Preservation and Sustainability"; and Section 11, "Lifelong Learning").

However, the resolution of the nation's debate about reform of the health care system marks only the first phase of a far-reaching shift from medical care to health protection and promotion. Effective efforts to provide preventive and primary care to those at greatest risk will necessarily be rooted in the communities where people live and work. The greatest deficits are in our central cities. Some examples of community-based services that are also labor intensive are: health education; family planning; universal immunization of children; efforts to reduce violence; programs to rid the community of drugs; care and nurturing of the frail elderly, victims of AIDS and the homebound; pre-natal and post-natal care for mothers and infants, preschool children and adolescents. Most are tasks best performed by people from the community, properly trained and supervised. These preventive measures have great potential to increase job levels where they are most needed, in ways that provide permanent benefits to people and communities.

10.

SOUND GOVERNMENT FINANCE

JOBS FOR ALL requires that the deficit and policies to reduce it be seen in perspective. The country has many economic problems, but the deficit is not the main one. Nor is it the cause of our economic problems. And contrary to a widespread view, eliminating the deficit is not a precondition for resolving other important economic problems. Deficit fixation and attempts to cut the deficit too deeply and too quickly can paralyze efforts to bring about much needed domestic change, drag the economy down, increase unemployment and actually increase the deficit itself. Policies to reduce unemployment in a growing economy will reduce the deficit. We must keep our focus on the culprit, unemployment, and start on the road to full employment.

Gaining a Realistic Perspective on the Deficit

Borrowing per se is not necessarily bad. Corporations borrow in the form of bonds and people borrow in the form of mortgages and educational loans. An important consideration is the object of the borrowing. It is one thing to borrow to pay for housing or education and another to go into debt for alcohol or narcotics. Nor is incurring a deficit for military overkill the same as incurring it for infrastructure repair and construction. Some borrowing is wasteful and destructive, other kinds contribute to the long-term health and growth of the person, community or nation. Another factor to consider is whether the borrower can keep up with the payments. If income grows, mortgage payments become less and less burdensome, but with job loss, the debt burden may become unsustainable. In a high growth, high wage economy, the burden of the deficit would be substantially reduced.

One way of gaining perspective on the deficit is to consider its origins in the fiscal policies of the Reagan Administration. The present federal deficit was created by a combination of government policies: massive tax cuts in 1981 that resulted in a decline in revenues as a proportion of GDP and a more than doubling of military expenditures. There was a concurrent decline in some social welfare spending which, though it wreaked havoc on the poor, did not offset the combination of revenue losses and defense increases.

The Reagan tax cuts, which disproportionately benefited the rich, were justified as a stimulus to investment. But instead of increasing productive investment, these tax giveaways fueled stock market and real estate speculation, wasteful mergers and buyouts and led to skyrocketing real estate costs. Robert S. McIntyre has estimated that the cost to the federal treasury in 1992 of tax cuts enacted since the late 1970s for the richest one percent of families was around $164 billion— $84 billion in decreased revenues and $81 billion in interest on the accumulated debt. Most of this cost was due to the tax changes enacted during the Reagan Administration. The recent revision of the tax code under the Clinton Administration is a shift in the right direction but does not go nearly far enough to redress the problem. Another less well-recognized outcome of the Reagan fiscal policies is that instead of taxing the wealthy to pay their fair share of public finance, government now borrows from them to finance its deficit. Thus, the wealthy received a double bonanza from the tax reductions of the eighties. We recommend a return to more progressive taxation. Kevin Phillips, for example, points out that revenue burdens similar to those of the Eisenhower era (14-15 percent of GNP) collected in non-payroll taxes might have prevented some of our fiscal problems.

One argument that is used for focusing on deficit reduction is that the deficit pushes up interest rates. The fact is that during the 1980s when the deficit shot up, interest rates did not rise. Studies by both the Congressional Budget Office (CBO) and the Brookings Institution have failed to find strong evidence linking deficits and interest rates. (There is a much stronger link between Federal Reserve policies and interest rates.) Finally, the size of the deficit is not a drag on the economy. When business does not expand it is because of lack of demand, not the deficit.

Perspective on the budgetary obsession can also be gained from recognizing that the current deficit is not very large relative to the size of the economy. The sum may be large, but the percent of GDP is the figure to watch. In 1945, due to the unprecedented size of wartime expenditures, the federal deficit was more than 22 percent of GDP, compared to the 5 percent that was projected for 1993. We are not suggesting a deficit of that magnitude. We are only pointing out that relative to the size of the economy, the 1945 deficit, albeit acquired in very unusual circumstances, was much larger than today's.

Reducing the deficit has its place, but it is all too easy to forget the toll that fixation on the deficit has taken in the past. In 1937, during the Great Depression, President Franklin Roosevelt, believing recovery was at hand, was anxious to balance the budget, eliminate deficit financing and cut government spending sharply. This, following on the heels of restrictive monetary policies instituted by an inflation-jittery Federal Reserve Board, led to a depression within a depression. Unemployment soared by three million within a year—from 14 percent in 1937 to 19 percent in 1938. Business activity contracted sharply, by nearly one half, and GNP plummeted. The unemployment and resulting loss of production that can ensue from such budget cutting is a far worse drain on an economy than the deficit.

Weimar Germany's response to the Depression is an even more tragic example of deficit fixation. Though unemployment among union members had skyrocketed—to 44 percent in 1932—the Weimar government remained traumatized by memories of hyperinflation in the early 1920s. To the bitter end, it pursued classic deflationary policies designed to balance the budget and reduce government expenditures. It never adopted trade-union economist W.S. Woytinksy's bold anti-unemployment plan designed to step up government spending on public works and to expand the money supply. Mass unemployment thus paved the road to Nazism. Once in power, Hitler destroyed the unions and then borrowed liberally from the Woytinsky plan—adding more than a few ideas of his own.

Unemployment and the Deficit

It cannot be stressed too much that unemployment itself adds considerably to the deficit. When unemployment rises, most of the shortfall in federal revenues comes from declining incomes of taxpayers. Jobless persons pay fewer taxes, as do companies that experience falling profits or go under completely. Rising unemployment also leads to more government expenditures on unemployment compensation, food stamps and other social programs, as well as increased outlays for interest to service the additional debt.

Extrapolating from CBO figures shows that a first year rise of one percentage point in the unemployment rate would have added about $45 billion to the deficit in fiscal year 1993 alone. If unemployment were to remain at that rate through FY 1998, the amount added to the deficit in that year alone would rise to $66 billion—most of the increase attributable to the mounting cost of servicing the accumulated debt. Using CBO figures we also find the cumulative cost to the federal treasury of a one point increase in unemployment *sustained* over five years, from FY 1994 to FY 1998, would be an astounding $289 billion. That is a significant proportion of the $500 billion budget deficit package that was negotiated in 1993. Thus, reducing unemployment turns out to be a potent way to reduce the deficit.

The Humphrey-Hawkins Full Employment and Balanced Growth Act of 1978 called for an *interim* goal of reducing the jobless rate to four percent within five years. If even that modest goal were set now, the impact on deficit reduction would be dramatic and would obviate the need to slash much-needed programs. We therefore advocate setting unemployment-reduction goals as a means of deficit reduction. Indeed, a growing full employment economy is an economy in which the deficit would disappear as an issue.

Since restrictive Federal Reserve policies have often contributed to unemployment and so to the deficit, the "Fed" should be held accountable and its policies made to conform to the unemployment-reduction goal. Fiscal and monetary policies need to be coordinated and focused on the reduction of unemployment.

America's Other "Deficits"

Unemployment itself creates other deficits—a human deficit and a tremendous loss of potential national output as well. For example, according to the CBO, if unemployment had been 5.5 percent in FY 1992 instead of 7.3 percent, the nation would have benefited from an additional $271 billion GDP—more than $1,000 for each man, woman and child. As Robert Eisner of Northwestern University, former President of the American Economic Association, put it in 1992: "We are literally throwing away potential output at the rate of $300 billion per year because of our current recession." Eisner is also eloquent regarding the deficits that are more serious than the budgetary shortfall. As he points out, over the long run, our deficits are in our rundown infrastructure of roads, bridges, airports, waste disposal facilities and lack of environmental protection. They are also in our failure to combat crime and drugs and in a significant part of a generation growing up semiliterate, in an unending cycle of poverty. Eisner notes that they are also in an educational system that is more and more clearly behind those found in the world's other developed nations. The real deficits, Eisner concludes, "are found in our growing gaps in child care and health care and in inadequate housing for tens of millions of Americans. These are our real deficits. They are large. They pose awesome dangers to the future of our economy and our nation."

Aside from the human waste that unemployment represents, our failure to invest in the infrastructure is a failure to take the steps that are necessary to restore economic growth. The infrastructure undergirds all economic activity. For decades we have let our infrastructure decay. According to the Office of Management and Budget (OMB), federal investment in public capital was cut by a third from 1976 to 1990. As Robert Heilbroner has pointed out, we have a unique opportunity (unlike other advanced industrial nations today) to stimulate our economy simply by catching up with our competition in the area of public capital: high speed railroad networks, non-polluting and efficient public transportation systems, bridges and dams, sewer systems, air traffic control networks, communications "highways," recycling and reuse centers, research and development centers. We recommend targeted tax credits for capital expenditures that would contribute to environmentally sustainable economic growth as well as job creation.

Altering Political Discourse on the Deficit

A budget deficit that a number of observers believe was created precisely to discourage domestic spending is doing just that. In this sense, the thoroughly predictable deficit—created by a reduction in revenues and an increase in military spending—is a success. It is important for those who recognize the deficit hysteria for what it is to attempt to alter the deficit fixation of our political discourse.

Reform of government accounting procedures would help us to recognize the difference between consumption expenditures and investment expenditures that contribute to productivity and, in time, to the public treasury. Such expenditures include education and training, civilian research and development, and physical infrastructure. As Robert Heilbroner points out, the federal budget, unlike the budget of any corporation and those of most other industrialized nations, fails to make the important distinction between operating and capital expenditures. Such a reform would help us to reconceptualize the deficit problem and to break its stranglehold on public investment policies that would have immense social and economic benefits to the nation.

Having demonstrated that the deficit is *not* the major economic problem, we nevertheless believe there are reasons to reduce it. The interest on the federal debt is an increasing government expense that is competing with other non-defense discretionary spending, a category which includes housing subsidies and other non-entitlement programs for the poor, as well as civilian research and development. Whereas non-defense discretionary spending fell from 24.5 percent of the federal budget in 1980 to under 16 percent in 1990, the cost of interest on the deficit rose from 8.5 percent to 14 percent in the same period. The major way to reduce our several deficits, we repeat, is for government to invest in our human and productive resources and to reverse the tax and military spending policies of the 1980s.

11.

LIFELONG LEARNING

The U.S. economy is now in a period of fundamental transition, a consequence of global integration, demilitarization, decades of environmental abuse and the shift to a national health care system. In this transition, millions of people will have to be retrained if they are to remain in the labor force. In addition, many young people lack the education and training necessary for entry into a changing labor market. Indeed, many human resource experts predict that in the emerging labor market people will be required to change their occupations five or six times during their lifetimes. Yet neither public nor private institutions have done much to prepare the workforce for this possibility.

What Is Wrong With the Current Approach to Training

The restructuring we have discussed will require changes in the education and training programs for people of all ages and at all levels. According to Labor Secretary Robert Reich, current training programs are totally inadequate to the need. Not only does our country spend less on training than our leading industrial competitors, but it is particularly neglectful of the training needs of line workers. Former Secretary of Labor Ray Marshall has pointed out that American companies spend between 1 and 2 percent of company payrolls on training, with two-thirds going for management, while companies in other industrial countries spend up to 6 percent of their payrolls on training and devote a significant share to frontline workers. Less than 10 percent of American non-college-educated workers receive any formal training. In contrast, a majority of the German workforce goes through some kind of apprenticeship program, and both Germany and Sweden have extensive retraining for already established workers. The American Society of Training and Development has reported that U.S. employees with college degrees are 50 percent more likely to receive training than non-college graduates, and executives with post-graduate degrees are twice as likely to get training as those with college degrees.

Businesses and government need to give more attention to training, particularly to meet the needs of low-income urban and rural youth whose education has not prepared them to enter the labor market. Elsewhere in this document (see Section 9, "Rebuilding the Nation's Cities") we have cited one kind of program that could begin to make a difference for unemployed inner-city youth. Other kinds of programs are also needed—for example, an expansion of the apprenticeship model well beyond the traditional U.S. focus on the building and metal trades. Sumner Rosen, retired Professor of Social Policy at Columbia University, points out that many of the technical jobs in the biomedical field are ones in which the basic skills could be learned in junior high and high school. By linking hospitals and biomedical firms with the schools, programs of earning while learning could be initiated which would provide young people not only with important skills for jobs that actually exist, but with the connections to the job networks that are so crucial to entering the labor market.

We applaud the Clinton Administration's recognition of the need for expanded training programs, including apprenticeship programs for young people, but the discussion still seems limited in three respects: first, it fails to comprehend the extent of the employment shifts that are taking place and hence the range of established workers (beyond displaced industrial workers) who are likely to be in need of retraining; second, it fails to appreciate the necessity of government and community planning for the shift to a different mix of industries; and third, it sees retraining, rather than job creation, as the solution to unemployment and underemployment.

We have called elsewhere for special "conversion" programs for workers displaced by military downsizing, by the restructuring of the health care system and by the transition to an environmentally sustainable economy (see Section 5, "Military Conversion;" Section 6,

"Environmental Preservation and Sustainability"; Section 9, "Rebuilding the Nation's Cities"). In addition to these sectors, there may be others that are hit at different times as the economy is restructured. In the long run, the transition from high-tech, capital intensive health care delivery and energy use to less capital intensive, decentralized, preventive and energy conserving industries is likely to produce more jobs. Nonetheless, the need for transitional planning and support will be critical.

A 1993 study by the U.S. Inspector General for the Labor Department acknowledges the failures of the current retraining program for workers hurt by foreign trade. These failures will be repeated in any new program if training is not accompanied by new job creation. Government must accept the reality that at this time jobs are not available for all of the retrained. And government must assume the responsibility of creating jobs for workers, not merely workers for jobs—often jobs that do not exist. One training model which we would be well-advised to consider is the successful on-the-job training programs initiated during World War II. Millions of women throughout the country were brought into the shops and trained to do highly skilled work. A system based on job-guaranteed training would create security and stability in our society. In all circumstances, job opportunity must be available at the conclusion of the training, lest training costs be wasted and discouragement abetted.

The Inspector General's study also found that retraining had little effect on raising wages for those workers obtaining new jobs. Raising workers' wages will require strong government and union efforts to halt the decline of the labor movement and of workers' influence generally (see Section 3, "Rights of Workers").

New Careers for Working Americans

In addition to the short-term retraining programs for displaced workers and apprenticeship and other programs for young people, the government needs to respond more comprehensively to the shifting nature of the labor market brought about by advanced technologies and global restructuring. To meet the need for lifelong learning opportunities, we propose a program of New Careers for Working Americans which would be both empowering to workers and beneficial to society.

This program would provide people displaced from jobs or family care with up to four years of tuition-free education and/or training at an approved institution of their own choosing. Workers would choose the educational or training program that best fit their needs within broad eligibility guidelines. The New Careers Program might involve a relatively short period of retraining with a specific vocational objective in view. But it would also provide the option for a fundamental shift in careers that would be possible only through an extended program of study, such as a college degree or some form of professional or technical certification.

Job counseling should be available throughout the program and at its completion, along with career relocation services. President Clinton's proposal for a one-stop counseling and referral service for displaced workers is a step in the right direction.

Another option in the New Careers program would be periodic sabbaticals for workers to undertake further study to enhance job-related skills and achieve personal enrichment. There are a number of possible variations to the basic plan. For example, if workers had an option of being employed part-time at their existing jobs, they might go to school part-time, with the balance of their compensation coming from this program. Yet another possible variation—if a worker participating in the program wanted to become a craftsperson—would be a period of apprenticeship to a recognized master of that particular craft.

The New Careers Program is solidly rooted in twentieth century public policy, notably the GI Bill, which enabled millions of World War II veterans to receive tuition-free education and living allowances and contributed to the post-war economic boom. Nonetheless, the program we propose represents a fundamental shift or extension in public policy in at least four ways: first, it recognizes education as work; second, it provides an opportunity for workers displaced from declining industries or those undergoing changes in occupational structure to prepare themselves for new occupations; third, it recognizes family care as a form of work and treats those who have completed these obligations as displaced workers; and fourth, it provides these workers with real choices in shaping the balance of their working lives.

All this makes the New Careers Program a means of empowerment for working people. But it also represents a means of nurturing what many thoughtful observers believe is our greatest national asset in a rapidly changing post-industrial world—namely, a well-trained labor force.

A program of lifelong learning must be grounded in basic primary and secondary education that effectively and meaningfully prepares future generations for the world of work. Yet, as is widely recognized today, American schools are not performing that function. Reforming public education in our society is a complex and extremely difficult task—and one that is absolutely vital to achieving our goal of JOBS FOR ALL. We recognize the importance of tackling this problem, but we do not attempt to deal with it here. Other initiatives are already addressing this issue. The reform of public education is an important aspect of an overall job strategy that impacts on many other social issues which affect and are affected by the world of work, such as economic and social inequality and racial, ethnic and gender discrimination. Vigorous implementation of the strategies outlined in this book, while hardly solving these long-standing failures in our society, will help to alleviate some of their more egregious manifestations.

New Careers for Working Americans would not only increase productivity but would have some other cost offsetting attributes. Among these would be reductions in the expenditures for unemployment insurance and public assistance, as well as for law enforcement and incarceration. From those who are able to maintain income during retraining, there would also be returns in the form of taxes to the federal treasury, not to mention the returns in future productivity and well-being.

CONCLUSION: MOVING TOWARD FULL EMPLOYMENT AND ECONOMIC JUSTICE

The authors of JOBS FOR ALL include veterans of earlier struggles for full employment. We are academics and social activists who have been close to the labor movement, the civil rights movement and the peace movement. We are united in believing that the major deprivation faced by millions of Americans is the denial of decent jobs at decent wages. A nation that intones the work ethic has the ethical obligation to provide an opportunity for gainful and productive employment to all within its borders.

But beyond that, as the most powerful nation in the world, we also have the moral, as well as practical, obligation to promote policies that move us toward global full employment. In view of the enormous unmet needs of the majority of the world's people for the most basic necessities, it is a shameful contradiction that there is also growing unemployment around the world. A sound international economy cannot be built on this contradiction. We have already suggested some principles and directions needed in the global economy. More solutions must be found that include international as well as national measures to increase the employment and living standards of people in poor as well as developed countries, especially those at the bottom. We cannot afford policies that have the effect of pitting workers in all countries against each other on a downward spiral. We recognize that international solutions will take even more time and political effort than domestic ones. Nevertheless, the tremendous power of capital in the new global economy should not paralyze our will to change domestic policies.

The authors of JOBS FOR ALL are aware that setting forth a policy or program, however coherent and compelling, is only the first step toward political change. Yet, we believe that articulating our ideas in this way is an important first step and itself a significant political action. Prepared under the auspices of New Initiatives for Full Employment (NIFE), this document is being used politically to gain support for an entitlement to work for all Americans.

Persuasion, or the ability to convince others to support an idea, a policy or a program is central to the political process. In this document we have attempted to persuade the reader that unemployment is a larger and more pervasive social problem than our political leaders are willing to admit, and one that gives rise to other grave problems that are undermining our people and institutions. We maintain that full employment is compatible with the nation's basic values and its deepest strivings, and that it remains an achievable goal, even in the new and complex world economy that is emerging.

As we move toward the twenty-first century and the end of this millenium, the prospect of jobs for all, we have argued, remains the centerpiece of a program for economic justice. We have maintained that the barriers to full employment are primarily political, not economic, but showing that full employment is economically feasible can help us overcome some of these political obstacles.

To argue persuasively is one way for the proponents of an idea or program to convince others to accept it, but so is the endorsement of individuals and groups who enjoy the respect and trust of the public. The endorsement of such individuals and groups can lend legitimacy and garner support for a political program. Even as we begin, the supporters of full employment include experts with impressive credentials and achievements. One such supporter is William Vickrey, former President of the American Economic Association, whose endorsement of full employment we cited in our summary. Such eminent economists as John Kenneth Galbraith, Robert Heilbroner, and the late Robert Lekachman are among those who have also associated themselves with the idea of full employment, and with NIFE.

It is NIFE's plan to increase the persuasiveness of this document by seeking a wide range of endorsers: academics, policymakers at all levels of government, religious and civic leaders, and organizations reflecting the diversity of interests that would be served by this broadly-defined program. NIFE members have already spoken about this program in public forums, contributed Op-Ed pieces and more reflective articles to newspapers and journals, and are available to speak, lead workshops or otherwise engage the public in a discussion of the issues.

Even as we complete this document, the effort to secure endorsements is underway. Indeed, those who have read earlier versions have offered their suggestions, and their ideas have already been incorporated. The individuals and organizations to whom we have circulated JOBS FOR ALL are also being asked to join us in promulgating it. We are asking them to endorse the general program and to work toward the enactment of those specific parts that are relevant to their individual and organizational goals, including the development of legislation and the recruitment of sponsors for it. We urge those who read this document to convey their reactions and suggestions to us and, if possible, to endorse and support it. Indeed, if the circulation of JOBS FOR ALL serves to bring us together, it will have contributed toward the birth of a social movement that is strong enough to put full employment on the political agenda.

In addition to setting forth our ideas, promulgating them and seeking endorsers and supporters, NIFE is also planning some specific legislative and other types of initiatives. The program that we have outlined is a broad one that includes proposals for the creation of jobs; raising the minimum wage; making the workplace more compatible with family life and women's occupational achievement; expanding workplace and civil rights; improving the employment opportunities of minorities, women and other disadvantaged workers; restoring the public infrastructure; strengthening public finance; ensuring corporate accountability; and furthering conservation and environmental protection.

Such a program has the advantage of appealing to a very wide constituency and encouraging the diverse members of this constituency to regard full employment as a means of fulfilling their own goals. We believe there is hardly a social problem that would not be reduced or made easier to solve if there were JOBS FOR ALL at decent pay. We intend to build a broad JOBS FOR ALL coalition by convincing those concerned with a wide range of serious social problems that they have a great deal to gain from the full employment program we propose.

Legislative and Other Initiatives

We have attempted to show the relationships among the diverse proposals made in JOBS FOR ALL, but we recognize that the enactment of such a complex program will require a great deal of adjustment and articulation between its parts. Given the political realities we face, the program will have to be struggled for piece by piece. It will require, not only winning the commitment of our own policymakers to fundamental changes in the way in which the economy is run, but a great deal of international adjustment as well. While the enactment of any of the domestic initiatives we have proposed is compatible with full employment, there are certain parts of the program that bear directly on its realization. It is therefore important to prioritize the proposals that have been made, and to develop a legislative strategy that would move us toward full employment.

Much will depend on the preferences of the policymakers who ally themselves with these ideas, but we think it important to suggest some legislative and other initiatives directly related to full employment. One such new initiative would be the introduction of an omnibus Full Employment and Economic Justice bill that would incorporate many of the ideas of JOBS FOR ALL. Its introduction by one or more legislators would lend credibility to the ideas articulated in JOBS FOR ALL, as well as give new visibility to the goal of full employment.

A second initiative would be to seek support for a permanent, standby job creation program. We recommend a program that would begin by creating jobs for half the unemployed, with a view toward complete coverage of the jobless. It seems to us important to introduce the idea of an entitlement to work, a goal which requires that in time all of the jobless be included. Some would argue that only a modest program is viable, but we are inclined to think that if a program is meager, its support will be too. President Clinton's stimulus package, which would have covered only a small fraction of the officially unemployed, inspired a filibuster by political opponents but little public enthusiasm.

A third new initiative would be the proposal of a high-level government Commission to Study and Propose Solutions to the Problem of Unemployment and Underemployment. This commission could hold hearings in various parts of the nation, consult with experts, take testimony from the unemployed and underemployed and report its findings and recommendations to the nation. It would contribute to public recognition of the problem of unemployment and hence to support for a more vigorous effort to expand employment opportunity. We will be seeking sponsorship in either the executive or legislative branch of government for such a commission.

A fourth initiative would increase public awareness of the true magnitude of joblessness and aid in planning JOBS FOR ALL. We will seek support for a new, expanded measure of unemployment. It would include, not just the official unemployed and those currently classified as discouraged workers, but also *all* others who want to work or are working part time involuntarily. In developing such a measure, we recommend that the Bureau of Labor Statistics call a conference of all interested groups, including those whose unemployment is most severely undercounted.

Recognizing that in a globally interdependent economy it would be difficult, if not impossible, to create full employment in one nation, and that a global "New Deal" is needed, a final, albeit long-range, **initiative** would be to call for a global employment summit, perhaps under the auspices of the United Nations. Such a summit, however, should go beyond the kind of meeting represented by the G7 Summit on Jobs convened by President Clinton in Detroit in 1994. That summit included only the finance and labor ministers from the industrialized countries. Predictably, it produced little in the way of sustantive proposals for reduction of unemployment, much less genuine global full employment. The initiative we call for should include representatives of both industrialized and developing nations. In addition to government ministers, representatives of nongovernmental organizations should also be included, such as: trade unions and other workers' organizations; organizations of the unemployed, of women and of the disabled; grassroots community development organizations; producer and consumer organizations; environmental organizations; advocates of disarmament and military conversion; and youths whose futures depend on jobs. The task of such a summit should be to translate the vast unmet needs of the world's people into effective aggregate demand by matching those needs to productive and socially meaningful jobs.

Until all Americans have the right to decent jobs, the American dream and American democracy itself remain an illusion. And until we have a global "New Deal" that raises the living standards of the world's poorest, while protecting the fragile environment, the future of life itself hangs in the balance. Let all those who seek to secure these economic rights join us in creating JOBS FOR ALL.

SELECTED REFERENCES

Abraham, Katherine G. 1983. "Structural/Frictional vs. Deficient Demand Unemployment." *American Economic Review* 73 (September): 708-724.

Advisory Council on Unemployment Compensation. 1994. Report and Recommendations transmitted to the President and Congress. Washington, D.C.

AFL-CIO Economic Research Department. 1993. "Ending Foreign Tax Loopholes: An Issue of Jobs and Tax Fairness." *AFL-CIO Reviews the Issues.* Report No. 70, prepared by Robert Lucore (December).

_____. 1993. *The 1993 Budget Debate: Cutting Through the Maze* (February).

Anderson, Marion. 1978. *The Empty Pork Barrel: Unemployment and the Pentagon Budget.* Lansing, MI: Public Interest Research Group.

Americans for Democratic Action. 1993. *A Liberal Economic Program for the Nineties.* Washington, DC: Americans for Democratic Action.

Aschauer, David Alan. 1990. *Public Investment and Private Sector Growth.* Washington, DC: Economic Policy Institute.

Ashford, N.A., and C. Caldart. 1991. *Technology, Law, and the Working Environment.* New York: Van Nostrand Reinhold.

A Shift in Military Spending to America's Cities: A Report for the United States Conference of Mayors. 1988. Lansing, MI: Employment Research Associates.

Barnet, Richard J., and John Cavanagh. 1994. *Global Dreams: Imperial Corporations and the New World Order.* New York: Simon & Schuster.

Barnet, Richard J. 1969. *The Economy of Death*. New York: Atheneum.

Beveridge, William H. 1944. *Full Employment in a Free Society*. London: Allen & Unwin.

Bowles, Samuel, David M. Gordon and Thomas E. Weisskopf. 1990. *After the Wasteland: A Democratic Economics for the Year 2000*. Armonk, NY: M.E. Sharpe.

Bradsher, Keith. 1992. "Trade Pact Job Losses Put at 150,000." *New York Times* (September 11): D1.

Brecher, Jeremy. 1993. "Global Unemployment at 700 Million." *Z Magazine* (November):45-48.

Brenner, Elsa. 1994. "Statistics Offer No Solace to Those in the Unemployment Line," *New York Times* (February 13): Sec. 13, p. 1.

Brenner, M. Harvey. 1976. *Estimating the Costs of National Economic Policy: Implications for Mental and Physical Health and Aggression*. Study prepared for the Joint Economic Committee of Congress. Washington, DC: U.S. Congress, 94th Congress, 2nd Session.

Breslow, Marc. 1993. "How Free Trade Fails." *Dollars and Sense*, No. 180 (October):6-9.

"Bronx Youth Conservation Corps." undated. c/o Save a Generation, St. Martin of Tours Roman Catholic Church, 664 Grote Ave., Bronx, N.Y. 10460.

Brown, Lester R., Christopher Flavin and Sandra Postel. 1991. *Saving the Planet*. New York: W.W. Norton & Co.

Bullock, Paul. 1981. *CETA at the Crossroads: Employment Policy and Politics*. Los Angeles: University of California Institute of Industrial Relations Monograph and Research Series 29.

Collins, Sheila D. 1991. "Persisting Unemployment and the Crisis of World Paradigm Shift." *International Journal of Sociology and Social Policy*, 11, No. 1, 2, 3 (Summer): 159-170.

————. 1989. "The New Opening for a Full Employment Movement." In D. Stanley Eitzen and Maxine Baca Zinn, eds., *The Reshaping of America: Social Consequences of the Changing Economy*. Englewood Cliffs, NJ: Prentice-Hall.

Commission on Employment Issues in Europe. 1989. *A Program for Full Employment in the 1990s: Report of the Kreisky Commission on Employment Issues in Europe*. Oxford: Pergamon Press.

Curtis, Lynn. 1993. *Investing in Children and Youth*. Washington, DC: The Milton S. Eisenhower Foundation.

Daniels, Lee A. 1991. "With Military Set to Thin Ranks, Blacks Fear They'll Be Hurt Most." *New York Times* (August 7): A1.

Defense Monitor. 1993. Vol. XXII, No. 4. Washington, DC: Center for Defense Information.

De Grasse, Robert. 1983. *Military Expansion, Economic Decline: The Impact of Military Spending on U.S. Economic Performance.* Armonk, NY: M.E. Sharpe.

_____. 1983. "Military Spending and Jobs." *Challenge* (July/August).

Dembo, David, and Ward Morehouse. 1993. *The Underbelly of the U.S. Economy: Joblessness and the Pauperization of Work in America.* New York: The Apex Press.

DePalma, Anthony. 1993. "Mexicans Fear for Corn, Imperiled by Free Trade." *New York Times* (July 12):2.

DeParle, Jason. 1994. "Report to Clinton Sees Vast Extent of Homelessness." *New York Times* (February 17):1.

duRivage, Virginia L. 1991. "New Policies for the Part-time and Contingent Workforce," briefing paper (November). Washington, DC: Economic Policy Institute.

Eisner, Robert. 1992. "Deficits: Which, How Much and So What?" *American Economic Review Papers and Proceedings* (May).

_____. 1991. "Our Real Deficits." *Journal of the American Planning Association.* 57, No. 2 (Spring).

Faux, Jeff. 1994. "Does America Have the Answer?" Paper delivered at an International Seminar on Growth and Employment, Magdalen College (April 14-15).

_____. 1994. *Joblessness and Wage Decline in Advanced Countries: Is There a Collective Solution?* (March 11). Washington, DC: Economic Policy Institute.

_____. 1993. "The Failed Case for NAFTA: The Ten Most Common Claims for the North American Free Trade Agreement and Why They Don't Make Sense." Statement of Jeff Faux, President of the Economic Policy Institute before Congress. *Congressional Record.* (June 30):A8333.

_____, and Thea Lee. 1992. *The Effect of George Bush's NAFTA on American Workers: Ladder Up or Ladder Down?* Washington, DC: Economic Policy Institute. (July).

Feldman, Jonathan, Robert Krinksy, and Seymour Melman. 1990. *A Future for America and Its Cities: The Peace Dividend and Economic Conversion.* Washington, DC: National Commission for Economic Conversion and Disarmament.

Fordham Institute for Innovation in Social Policy. 1993. *The Index of Social Health.* Tarrytown, NY: Fordham University Graduate Center.

Freeman, Richard B. 1991. "Employment and Earnings of Disadvantaged Young Men." In Christopher Jencks and Paul E. Peterson, eds. *The Urban Underclass*. Washington, DC.: The Brookings Institution.

Galbraith, John Kenneth. 1992. *The Culture of Contentment*. Boston: Houghton Mifflin.

Gans, Herbert. B. 1990. "Planning for Work Sharing: The Promise and Problems of Egalitarian Work Time Reduction." In K. Erikson and S.P. Vallas, eds. *The Nature of Work: Sociological Perspectives*. New Haven: American Sociological Association Series and Yale University Press.

Ginsburg, Helen. 1993. "Preventing Unemployment: Values, Concepts and Policies in the United States, Germany, and Sweden." Unpublished paper presented to the International Conference, Society for the Advancement of Socio-Economics, New York, March 26-28.

_____. 1983. *Full Employment and Public Policy: The United States and Sweden*. Lexington, MA: Lexington Books.

_____. 1991. "Changing Concepts of Full Employment: Divergent Concepts, Divergent Goals." *International Journal of Sociology and Social Policy* 11, No. 1, 2, 3 (Summer):18-28.

_____. 1975. *Unemployment, Subemployment and Public Policy*. New York: New York University School of Social Work Center for Studies in Income Maintenance Policy.

Goldberg, Gertrude Schaffner, and Eleanor Kremen, eds. 1990. *The Feminization of Poverty: Only in America?* New York: Praeger.

Gross, Bertram. 1991. "From Fool Employment to Global Human Rights," *International Journal of Sociology and Social Policy,* 11, No. 1, 2, 3 (Summer):118-158.

Grossman, Richard L., and Richard Kazis. 1982. *Fear at Work: Job Blackmail, Labor and the Environment*. New York: The Pilgrim Press.

Hartmann, Heidi, and Roberta Spalter-Roth. 1993. *The Real Employment Opportunities of Women Participating in AFDC: What the Market Can Provide*. Washington, DC: Institute for Women's Policy Research (October 23).

Harvey, Philip. 1993. "Employment as a Human Right." In William J. Wilson, ed., *Sociology and the Public Agenda*. Newbury Park, CA: Sage.

_____. *1989. Securing the Right to Employment: Social Welfare*

Policy and the Unemployed in the United States. Princeton, NJ: Princeton University Press.

Heilbroner, Robert. 1992. "An Economy in Deep Trouble." *Dissent* (Fall): 445-450.

International Covenant on Economic, Social and Cultural Rights. 1966. G.A. Res. 2200, 21 U.N. GAOR, Supp. (No. 16) 49, U.N. Doc. A/6316.

International Labour Conventions and Recommendations, 1919-1981. Geneva: International Labour Office.

Jacobs, Michael. 1991. *The Green Economy: Environment, Sustainable Development and the Politics of the Future*. London: Pluto Press.

Karesek, Robert, and T. Theorell. 1990. *Healthy Work*. New York: Basic Books.

Kilborn, Peter T. 1993. "U.S. Study Says Job Retraining Is Not Effective." *New York Times* (October 15):1.

Lav, Iris, Marion Nichols, James St. George, and Robert Greenstein. 1993. *End of the Line: What the End of Emergency Unemployment Benefits Means*. Washington, DC: Center on Budget and Policy Priorities.

Lazere, Edward B., Paul Leonard, Catherine N. Dolbeare, and Barry Zigas. 1991. *A Place to Call Home: The Low Income Housing Crisis Continues*. Washington, DC: Center on Budget and Policy Priorities.

Lessin, Nancy. 1994. "Whistle Blowers' Rights: How Job Security Could Safeguard the Environment." *Dollars and Sense* (May-June):18-22ff.

Levitan, Sar A., and Elizabeth I. Miller. 1993. *The Equivocal Prospects for Indian Reservations*. Washington, D.C.: George Washington University Center for Policy Studies Occasional Paper No. 2.

_____ and Frank Gallo. 1992. *Spending to Save: Expanding Employment Opportunities*. Washington, DC: Center for Policy Studies, George Washington University.

_____, and Isaac Shapiro. 1987. *Working but Poor: America's Contradiction*. Baltimore, MD: Johns Hopkins University Press.

MacEwan, Arthur. 1991. "The New Evangelists: The Gospel of Free Trade." *Dollars and Sense*. No. 171 (November):6 ff.

Markusen, Ann, and Joel Yudken. 1992. *Dismantling the War Economy*. Basic Books.

McFate, Katherine. 1991. "First World Poverty." *Focus* (November):3-4.

McGeary, Michael G.H., and Laurence E. Lynn, Jr., eds. 1988. *Urban*

Change and Poverty. Washington, DC: National Research Council/National Academy Press.

McIntyre, Robert S. 1991. *Inequality and the Federal Deficit*. Washington, DC: Citizens for Tax Justice.

Mead, Walter Russell. 1994. "Altered States: Managing the Global Economy." *The American Prospect* (Winter):58-61.

Melman, Seymour. 1992. *Rebuilding America: A New Economic Plan for the 1990s*. Westfield, NJ: Open Magazine Pamphlet Series.

_____. 1989. "The Peace Dividend: What to Do with the Cold War Money." *New York Times*. (December 17).

_____. 1974. *The Permanent War Economy*. New York: Simon & Schuster.

_____. 1970. *Pentagon Capitalism: The Political Economy of War*. New York: McGraw-Hill.

Merva, Mary, and Richard Fowles. 1992. "Effects of Diminished Economic Opportunity on Social Stress: Heart Attacks, Strokes and Crime." Washington, DC: Economic Policy Institute.

Mishel, Lawrence, and Jared Bernstein. 1993. *The State of Working America 1992-93*. Economic Policy Institute Series. Armonk, NY: M.E. Sharpe.

Moberg, David. 1992. "Cutting the Military: How Low Can We Go?" *In These Times* (February 12-18).

Mucciaroni, Gary. 1990. *The Political Failure of Employment Policy, 1945-1982*. Pittsburgh: University of Pittsburgh Press.

National Labor Committee Education Fund in Support of Worker and Human Rights in Central America. 1993. *Free Trade's Hidden Secrets: Why We Are Losing Our Shirts* (November). New York: National Labor Committee Education Fund.

_____. 1992. *Paying to Lose Our Jobs* (September). New York: National Labor Committee Education Fund.

National Urban League Research Department. 1993. *Quarterly Economic Report on the African American Worker*. 33 (June).

Oravoc, John R. 1993. "Mexico Spends Millions to Sell NAFTA in U.S." *AFL-CIO News* (May 31).

Orshansky, Mollie. 1965. "Counting the Poor: Another Look at the Poverty Profile." *Social Security Bulletin* 28 (January):3-29.

Osberg, Lars. 1991. *Economic Inequality and Poverty: International Perspectives*. Armonk, NY: M.E. Sharpe, Inc.

Osterman, Paul. 1991. "Gains from Growth: The Impact of Full Employment on Poverty in Boston." In Chistopher Jencks and Paul E. Peterson, eds. *The Urban Underclass*. Washington, D.C.: The

Brookings Institution.

Peace Dividend. 1990. Newsletter of the Peace Dividend Movement 1, No. 2 (Summer).

Peterson, Wallace C. 1994. *Silent Depression: The Fate of the American Dream.* New York: W.W. Norton.

_____. 1992. "What is to be Done?" *Journal of Economic Issues* XXVI, No. 2 (June):337-348.

Pizzigati, Sam. 1992. *The Maximum Wage.* New York: The Apex Press.

Pollin, Robert. 1993. "Debt Obsessed." *Dollars and Sense*, No. 185 (April):20.

Prokesch, Stephen. 1993. "Service Jobs Fall as Business Gains." *New York Times* (April 18):43.

Renner, Michael. 1991. *Jobs in a Sustainable Economy.* Worldwatch Paper 104 (September). Washington, DC: Worldwatch Institute.

Rifkin, Jeremy. 1993. "The Clinton Dilemma." *Tikkun* 8, No. 3:14-79.

Rosen, Sumner M. 1993. "The Right to Employment," *Monthly Review* 1, No. 6 (November):1-10.

_____. 1993. "What About Welfare Fathers?" *New York Newsday* (June 28):38.

_____. 1992. "Protecting Labor Rights in Market Economies." *Human Rights Quarterly* 14:371-382.

Rosenthal, Marguerite G. 1990. "Sweden: Promise and Paradox." In Gertrude Schaffner Goldberg and Eleanor Kremen, eds. *The Feminization of Poverty: Only in America?* New York: Praeger, pp. 128-155.

Ruggles, Patricia. 1990. *Drawing the Line: Alternative Poverty Measures and Their Implications for Public Policy.* Washington, DC: The Urban Institute Press.

Saunders, Norman C. 1993. "Employment Effects of the Rise and Fall in Defense Spending." *Monthly Labor Review* (April):3 ff.

Schmid, Gunther, Bernd Reissert, and Gert Bruch. 1992. *Unemployment Insurance and Active Labor Market Policy: An International Comparison of Financing Systems.* Detroit: Wayne State University Press.

Schor, Juliet B. 1991. *The Overworked American: The Unexpected Decline of Leisure.* New York: Basic Books.

Schwarz, John E., and Thomas J. Volgy. 1992. *The Forgotten Americans.* New York: W. W. Norton.

Shapiro, Isaac, and Marion Nichols. 1992. *Far From Fixed: An Analysis of the Unemployment Insurance System.* Washington, DC: Center on Budget and Policy Priorities.

Shorter Work Time News. c/o Shorter Work Time Group, Women for Economic Justice, Boston, MA.

Silk, Leonard. 1991. "Getting the Benefit of Military Cuts." *New York Times* (September 20):D2.

Smeeding, Timothy M., and Lee Rainwater. 1991. *Cross-National Trends in Income, Poverty and Dependency: The Evidence for Young Adults in the 80s.* Working Paper 67 (August 19). Syracuse, NY: Center for Policy Research, Syracuse University.

Therborn, Göran. 1985. *Why Some Peoples Are More Employed Than Others: The Strange Paradox of Growth and Unemployment.* London: Verso.

Tidwell, Billy J. 1991. *Playing to Win: A Marshall Plan for America.* New York: National Urban League.

Tolchin, Martin. 1994. "Redirecting Technology to Travelers From Troops." *New York Times* (February 14):A10.

Trade Union Advisory Committee to the Organisation for Economic Cooperation and Development. 1993. "Trade Union Statement to the OECD Ministerial Council and Tokyo Summit" (July-August). Adopted at the TUAC Plenary Session, May 1993. Paris Trade Union Advisory Committee to the OECD.

Turgeon, Lynn. 1994. "The Forgotten Lessons of Keynes' Revolution." *Newsday* (March 13):42.

Uchitelle, Louis. 1993. "Three Decades of Dwindling Hope for Prosperity." *New York Times* (May 9):Sec. 4, p. 1.

_____. 1993. "Temporary Workers Are on the Increase in Nation's Factories." *New York Times* (July 6):D2.

Ullman, John E. 1990. "The Conversion Impact of Industrial Renewal and Economic Recovery." Unpublished paper presented at the Conference on Restructuring America, New Intiatives for Full Employment, New York City, March 23-24.

Universal Declaration of Human Rights. United Nations Document a/811, 1948.

U.S. Bureau of the Census. 1993. *Money Income of Households, Families, and Persons in the United States: 1992.* Series P-60, No. 184. Washington, DC: U.S. Government Printing Office.

_____. 1992. *Poverty in the United States.* Series P-60, No. 185. Washington, DC: U.S. Government Printing Office.

_____. 1992. *Workers with Lower Earnings: 1964 to 1990.* Series P-60, No. 178. Washington, DC: U.S. Government Printing Office.

U.S. Congress, Congressional Budget Office. 1990. *The Economic and Budget Outlook: Fiscal Years 1991-1995: A Report to the Senate and House Committees on the Budget,* Part I. Washington, DC: U.S. Government Printing Office.

_____. 1993. *The Economic and Budget Outlook: Fiscal Years 1994-1998.*

_____, Joint Economic Committee. 1993. *Potential Economic Impacts of the North American Free Trade Agreement: An Assessment of the Debate* (November).

U.S. Department of Labor, Bureau of Labor Statistics. 1993. "Briefing Materials on the Redesigned Current Population Survey" (December).

U.S. Department of Labor, Bureau of Labor Statistics. 1993. *Monthly Labor Review* (September).

U.S. Department of Labor, Inspector General. 1993. *Trade Adjustment Assistance Program: Audit of Program Outcomes in Nine States* (30 September).

Vickrey, William. 1993. "Today's Task for Economists." *American Economic Review* 83 (March):1-10.

Weir, Margaret. 1992. *Politics and Jobs: The Boundaries of Employment Policy in the United States.* Princeton, NJ: Princeton University Press.

Weltman, Eric. 1993. "Jobs Versus the Environment? No—The Real Choice is Between Toxic and Sustainable Economy." *Public Citizen* 13, No. 5 (Sept./Oct.):20-21.

Williams, Daniel, and Marc Breslow. 1992. "Can the Cities be Saved?" *Dollars and Sense*, No. 180 (October):12-14.

Wilson, William J. 1987. *The Truly Disadvantaged: The Inner City, the Underclass and Public Policy.* Chicago: University of Chicago Press.

_____, and Loic J.D. Wacquant. 1989. "Poverty, Joblessness, and the Social Transformation of the Inner City." In P. Cottingham and David Ellwood, eds., *Welfare Policy for the 1990s.* Cambridge, MA: Harvard Univerity Press, pp. 70-102.

Wykle, Lucinda, Ward Morehouse, and David Dembo. 1991. *Worker Empowerment in a Changing Economy: Jobs, Military Production and the Environment.* New York: The Apex Press.

Zelnick, Robert C. 1990. "We Could Easily Save $350 Billion." *New York Times* (February 12):A21.

Zinzer, Adolfo Aguilar. 1991. "Mexico: The Authoritarian Friend and Partner." *Peace and Democracy News* VI, No. 1 (Winter).

ABOUT THE AUTHORS

AND CONSULTANTS

SHEILA D. COLLINS is Associate Professor of Political Science at William Paterson College with a specialization in American politics, public policy and constitutional law. She also serves as a doctoral advisor to students at Walden University. Collins is a founding member of New Initiatives for Full Employment. She has been a consultant to the New York State Labor Department on affirmative action and to the New Jersey Council of Churches on economic policy. She is the recipient of a grant from the New World Foundation for work on full employment, from the Consortium for Worker Education for workplace education evaluation and from the Anita Mishler Foundation for education on economic change. Collins is the author of *A Different Heaven and Earth* (1974); and *The Rainbow Challenge: The Jackson Campaign and the Future of U.S. Politics* (1987). She is currently working on a book entitled, *Let Them Eat Ketchup! The Politics of Poverty and Inequality*. She has lectured in Canada, Great Britain, Italy, Sweden, and West Africa. Her articles on American politics, public policy and political culture have appeared in numerous collections and in such publications as *Harvard Educational Review*, the *International Journal of Sociology and Social Policy, Monthly Review* and *Social Policy*.

HELEN LACHS GINSBURG is Professor of Economics at Brooklyn College, City University of New York with specialties in labor and social welfare. She was involved in efforts to secure full employment legislation in the United States in the 1970s and is a founding member of New Initiatives for Full Employment. She has testified on employment issues to various congressional committees and has served as a consultant to religious, women's, social welfare and other groups working on employment and economic policy. Ginsburg was the recipient of a Swedish Bicentennial Fund travel research grant to study employment policy in Sweden and the Lawrence Klein award of the Bureau of Labor Statistics for her work on comparative employment. She was also a visiting research scholar at the *Wissenschaftszentrum* in Berlin. Ginsburg is the editor of *Poverty, Economics and Society* (1972, 1981); author of *Unemployment, Subemployment and Public Policy* (1975); and *Full Employment and Public Policy: The United States and Sweden* (1983). She is currently working on a book entitled, *Jobs for All: Rhetoric and Reality in the United States, Germany and Sweden.* Her articles and reviews have appeared in numerous collections and in such publications as the *Monthly Labor Review,* the *Industrial and Labor Relations Review, Policy Studies Journal, Policy Studies Review, Social Thought, The Nation, Jewish Currents* and *America.*

GERTRUDE SCHAFFNER GOLDBERG is Associate Professor and was, for a number of years, Director of the Center for Social Policy, Adelphi University School of Social Work. Her specialty is in social policy, particularly as it relates to women. She began her career as a social worker and program planner at Mobilization for Youth, the delinquency prevention program in New York that became the model for programs in the War on Poverty. She has been involved in the establishment and leadership of New Initiatives for Full Employment and in efforts to reorder national priorities through the vehicle of a "peace dividend." Goldberg was a keynote speaker at the Nordisk Forum '88, in Oslo, convened by the governments of the Nordic countries as a regional followup to the 1985 U.N. Conference on the Decade for Women in Nairobi. She has also lectured in other European countries and in Asia. Goldberg is the co-editor of *The Feminization of Poverty: Only in America?* (1990); and author of *Government Money for Everyday People: A Guide to Income Support Programs* (4th ed., 1991). Her articles on organizational change, the education of socially disadvantaged children and socially and economically vulnerable groups of women have appeared in numerous collections and in such publications as *Social Policy, Social Service Review* and *Social Work.*

CONSULTANTS

WARD MOREHOUSE is President of the Council on International and Public Affairs, Chairman of the Intermediate Technology Development Group of North America, and Research Associate in the Southern Asia Institute at Columbia University's School of International and Public Affairs.

LEONARD RODBERG is Associate Professor of Urban Studies and fellow of the Michael Harrington Center at Queens College, City University of New York.

SUMNER ROSEN is retired Professor of Social Policy at Columbia University and a Fullbright Scholar in 1989-1990 in Taiwan. He is a founding member of New Initiatives for Full Employment and Jews for Racial and Economic Justice.

JUNE ZACCONE is Associate Professor of Economics at Hofstra University, a member of New Initiatives for Full Employment, and active in the Northeast Chapter of The Other Economic Summit (TOES).

NEW INTIATIVES FOR FULL EMPLOYMENT
RESPONSE FORM

Please list me/us as ENDORSERS of JOBS FOR ALL IN A NATION THAT WORKS. (While I/we may not agree with every detail, I/we feel that JOBS FOR ALL points the way toward full employment and economic justice.)

INDIVIDUAL ENDORSEMENT

Signature_____

Printed name_____

Address_____Phone_____

_____Zip_____

Organization_____

Include as affiliation_____For identification only_____

ORGANIZATIONAL ENDORSEMENT

Name of organization_____

Address_____Phone_____

_____Zip_____

Contact Person(s)_____

_____I/we enclosed the names of others who should see JOBS FOR ALL.

_____I/we would like to work on the project of disseminating JOBS FOR ALL and building a movement for full employment.

_____I/we enclose a contribution to assist the distribution of JOBS FOR ALL.

$25_____ $50_____ $100_____ $1000_____ Other $_____

Please return this form to: New Intiatives for Full Employment, c/o Council on International and Public Affairs, 777 U.N. Plaza, Suite 3C, New York, N.Y. 10017.